ROBERT G. CLARK'S JOURNEY TO THE HOUSE

Robert G. Clark's Journey to the House

A BLACK POLITICIAN'S STORY

Will D. Campbell

University Press of Mississippi / Jackson

www.upress.state.ms.us

Copyright © 2003 by Will D. Campbell
Manufactured in the United States of America
Frontis: Photograph courtesy of Tougaloo College Archives
11 10 09 08 07 06 05 04 03   4 3 2 1

Library of Congress Cataloging-in-Publication Data

Campbell, Will D.
Robert G. Clark's journey to the house : a black politician's
story / Will D. Campbell.
p. cm.
Includes bibliographical references and index.
ISBN 1-57806-526-7 (alk. paper)
1. Clark, Robert George, 1929– 2. African American legislators—Mississippi—
Biography. 3. Legislators—Mississippi—Biography. 4. Mississippi. Legislature—
Biography. 5. Mississippi—Politics and government—1951– 6. African
Americans—Mississippi—Politics and government—20th century. 7. African
Americans—Civil rights—Mississippi—History—20th century. I. Title.
F345.3.C57 C36 2003
328.762'092—DC21
2002010166

British Library Cataloging-in-Publication Data available

PREFACE

In many circles it is assumed that Mississippi's people are the most homogeneous in the nation. Not long ago I started out to write a book about Mississippi heritage. Soon I discovered that I didn't know what that was.

When I was a child growing up on a small cotton farm in the Amite County hills during the years of the Great Depression, I didn't think much about heritage. I didn't have to, for mine was manifest in everyday life. Heritage was a country school that met in two rooms of the abandoned Woodmen Hall when twice the schoolhouse itself was burned. Part of the heritage was that we knew the arsonist was one of our own.

It, the heritage, was a Baptist church a few yards from the schoolhouse. There were no other churches of any declension in the community, so all students of the school, always fewer than two hundred, were Baptists. Church functions were also school functions. Although the teachers and administrators were staunch advocates of the First Amendment to the U.S. Constitution, in reality we were a parochial school. Separation of church and state had to do with schools across the Louisiana state line where, we heard, Catholic nuns taught in public schools. It did not apply to our principal, who was a part-time Baptist preacher. Nor did it have to do with the daily chapel service where the principal read a Scripture passage, gave a brief devotional, and said a prayer. There was no reason for dissent, for all of us, students and faculty alike, were not only Christian, not only Protestant, we were all Baptists. Most of us were kinfolk as well. There was not a Catholic on our side of McComb, not a Jew on our side of New Orleans, and not a Methodist or Presbyterian on our side of Liberty, the county seat and site of the post office and courthouse.

Our heritage was annual trips to McComb where we sold our cotton. It was orders for school clothes from Sears, Roebuck and Montgomery Ward catalogs. It was the annual summer revival where chickens were penned for two weeks of fattening to feed visiting preachers, revivals measured for success by how many children come of age joined the church and were baptized before winter in the crystal-clear waters of the Amite River. And how much money was paid to the visiting revivalist.

Our heritage had few outside influences. Occasionally traveling salesmen we called drummers came by to try to sell wrought-iron wood-burning stoves or burial insurance policies.

Our world was small so the notion of heritage was limited. The school had a meager library, probably no more than a hundred books, and when strangers tried to encroach on East Fork imprimatur they were quickly rebuffed. For example, my younger brother came home from school one day talking about the battle of Armageddon, quoting as authority a book by Charles Taze Russell and Judge Rutherford, telling us when the world would end and why we shouldn't salute the flag, join the army, or have a blood transfusion. A great-uncle who had been considered the village Nestor had been converted recently by some itinerant Jehovah's Witnesses and talked of nothing else. In an all-Baptist neighborhood that was not a mark of mental stability. The book was discussed by the Baptist Sanhedrin where it was determined that the converted, and thus mentally troubled, neighbor had bootlegged the book into the school library. The principal agreed that, of course, the book should not be in a public school library. This despite the fact that the Baptist Sunday school literature was regularly placed on the shelves and the following Sunday's lesson was discussed by the principal at each Friday chapel. When burning the book was suggested, the principal, more of a constitutionalist than he appeared on other issues, effected a compromise. He would instead put it on his compost pit where its demise would be certain but so gradual that no one could tell when it ceased to be a legible treatise.

All that was in the twenties and thirties, my early childhood, and did not last. In the mid and late thirties things began to change rapidly and our world expanded. The gravel road was paved, we began taking a daily newspaper, electricity from a federal program brought nighttime reading. A battery radio brought us news of a European war brewing. A primitive but workable telephone connected us with kinfolk as far away as New Orleans and Baton Rouge. Progress. Progress. All in the name of progress. Then the war came and all that had been our heritage was gone forever. Airplanes appeared, later television, and automobiles to take us to movie houses twenty miles away, places alien to our culture.

Heritage? What heritage?

All of-age males went off to war. First, for me, was Texas. Then Arkansas. Florida. California. Two years in the South Pacific. The war ended and those of us still alive scattered again, I to schools in North Carolina, Louisiana, Connecticut. Jobs here and there.

Where, now, does a Mississippi octogenarian go in search of his heritage? Not to East Fork. East Fork is no more. Subdivisions that were cotton fields harbor by night men and women who will be in Baton Rouge, Natchez, New Orleans, or Jackson by day, their young in day-care shelters wherever there is room.

There is, however, such a thing as Mississippi heritage. I began a search for it and soon discovered that it covers the state. And includes representatives from every continent and every race.

Although I left Mississippi more than sixty years ago I have never left it. I have buried there father, mother, grandsires and grandames of four generations, stretching back to before statehood. A brother, nephew, dozens, hundreds of kinfolk lie in the red clay of the piney woods country. But how now does one in his dotage sum it all up?

Listen to blues in the Delta, eat German food in Gluckstadt, watch the blessing of the fleet with Shrimp Queen contestants who are Slavonian, Acadian, Vietnamese, dance the Cajun two-step in Biloxi, visit the Museum of the Southern Jewish Experience near Utica, go to a Chinese-owned grocery store in a black neighborhood.

Trying to catalog the nationalities, religions, and cultures reminds one of the biblical story of Pentecost. There, the Book of Acts itemizes those from Parthia, Media, and Elam. Others are from Mesopotamia, Judea, Cappadocia, Pontus, Asia, Phrygia, Pamphylia, Egypt, parts of Libya near Cyrene, Rome, Crete, and Arabia.

The remarkable thing about the biblical legend is that everyone was speaking the same language. Dozens of tongues all melded into one.

A Mississippi Pentecost, maybe with Nanih Waiya as the gathering place, would include the Choctaws, Scots, English, Welsh, Irish, Africans, French, Cajuns, people from Mexico, Honduras, Colombia, Costa Rica, and Venezuela, Slavonians, Vietnamese, Lebanese, Italians, Indians, Chinese, Germans, Greeks, and many others. Unfortunately, a Mississippi Pentecost is not yet. (A common language. Perhaps a common flag?)

I was overwhelmed by Mississippi's diversity concerning a common heritage but did not despair.

By accident I met one man who, while not representing all nations, does represent all races.

I have chosen to deal with Mississippi heritage by writing the story of that one man. One of his great-grandfathers was a Creek Indian, as indigenous to Mississippi heritage as is possible. A great-great-grandfather was a southern planter, a white man whose name is unknown, as much of everyone's heritage is unknown. The women of his lineage were black.

The Creek nation. If it is correct that who we call American Indians had their beginning in Asia and crossed the Bering Strait to reach what eons later would be called America, he is of the Mongolian race. His great-great-grandfather was Caucasian. His grandmothers were Negroid. He at once puts the lie to the theory of race and authenticates some lines of an old southern folk song:

'Fore we was born we was all kin.
When we dead we'll be kinfolks again.

He epitomizes Mississippi's heritage in other ways as well.

He is of the land, living all his life on land his great-grandfather bought for a dollar an acre with money he had saved during the Civil War when other blacksmiths were at war and he was the only one left.

He is a man of the political realm, serving since 1967 in the state house of representatives where he is now speaker pro tempore.

He is a man of the church, an ordained Baptist clergyman.

He is a man of education and athletics. A graduate of Jackson State University with a master's degree from Michigan State University, he was for many years a teacher and coach in the public schools of Mississippi.

Since I met him five years ago I have followed his tracks from the halls of the legislature to the fields and woods of his farm in Holmes County, from his living room where I sipped tea with him and his wife, Jo Ann, to pulpits and lecture halls where he held forth with skill and abandon, from casual social gatherings to official venues where he presided over the most sensitive business of the state.

I followed him, and I listened. This narrative is the result of those many conversations. He has verified the facts concerning his life and times as I have written them here.

His name is Robert George Clark. This is his story. I will tell it as best I can, for it is the distillation of both his heritage and mine.

I

There was a strange quiet in Ebenezer. Not exactly tension; sort of wonderment. It was first Tuesday in November, election day in Mississippi. Voting day in Holmes County, Mississippi, was generally a drowsy end of a minor skirmish. Not so in 1967. It had been two years since the Voting Rights Act had been passed by Congress, but the effect of it was just beginning to reach rural counties in the Deep South. This was the year of testing. Black southerners were running for important offices, and many were voting for the first time. Still, this was Holmes County, Mississippi, a place not noted for electoral grace. Two years earlier not one black citizen was registered to vote.

Ebenezer was an ideal place for testing the new voting law. Named for the site of two decisive biblical battles, one in which the Israelites were decisively defeated by the Philistines and the other in which the Philistines were annihilated by the Israelites, this battle would be just as consequential for the future of America as those long-ago encounters between the forces of good and evil.

The village had been settled even before the signing of the

Treaty of Dancing Rabbit Creek, the document that opened the floodgates for European settlers.

Ebenezer, on Mississippi Highway 14, is about ten miles south of Lexington and ten miles northwest of Pickens. Originally it was located on the old coach road over which the pioneers passed on their way to take the boats in Yazoo City, then called Manchester. A Methodist church was there prior to the treaty, and the crafty Chief Greenwood Leflore translated the sermons for the soon-to-be-gone Choctaws. It had been an important place from its beginning. It was a relay station, Smith's Tavern, a place where all the frills of comfort and debauchery special to the frontier could be found. Horses, kept in readiness at all times, were bridled and harnessed, their heads always turned toward Yazoo.

Ebenezer was the birthplace of the late Perry Howard, a lawyer and for thirty-five years the Republican National Committeeman from Mississippi, one of the most influential Negro Republicans in his time.

It was also the home of Milton Olive III, a Negro soldier who was awarded the Congressional Medal of Honor for his service in Vietnam, where he had grabbed a hurled grenade with his hand and thrown his body on it, losing his own life but saving the lives of the other soldiers with him.

On this day in 1967, a neatly dressed, well-built, and handsome Negro man in his late thirties strolled purposely down the length of one of Ebenezer's two stores. He looked neither right nor left as he passed the compartment containing hundreds of spools of thread with J & P Coats labels, a counter displaying Baby Ruths, O'Henrys, and a dozen other candies, a cold drinks box with racks of empty, returnable bottles beside it, and the wide assortment of groceries, hardware, and dry goods still carried by village stores. On the walls were faded signs advertising various products, some no longer stocked: Putnam Dyes & Tints, Old North State Tobacco, Lydia E. Pinkham, Grove's Chill Tonic, Black Draught, and Carter's Little Liver Pills. He moved directly toward a row of canvas booths almost at the very end of the store. A round wooden block with deep scars of butchery had been moved aside to make room for the booths. Nearby was a meat case where local beef had been cut and racked.

Through an open door leading to a back room could be seen a tiny casket. On this particular and precarious day it might have seemed a subtle intimidation. Actually it was no more than part of an inventory of earlier years when the store sold coffins along with all other necessities of both life and death in rural Mississippi. Any more the coffin was used only for Halloween antics.

A sheriff's car was parked directly in front of the building with red lights flashing. Two uniformed and visibly armed deputies sat just inside the door. One on each side. Anyone entering or leaving the building had to pass directly between them. A drizzle of rain was falling. Through the sweated win-

dow the whirling lights made the whitish rain look like summer gnats swarming in the wind. The rain had begun before
midnight and had not let up.

Two lines of Negro men formed a sort of corridor in the
midsection of the store. They had been gathering inside the
store since the first light of day. There was a rhythmic shifting
of feet and frequent, barely audible throat clearings. The two
sounds, alternating, seemed a language.

At the very back of the room, near the door where the little
casket was visible, was a cluster of women. They were not in
formation but were clearly of one intent. They wore their Sunday clothes—dresses of voile, dotted swiss, and cotton of various prints and patterns. The majority wore their Sunday hats
as well. Some had baskets or brown paper bags of food—fried
chicken, ham biscuits, and sweet tea in Mason jars or thermos
jugs. An elderly woman held a blue Milk of Magnesia bottle
filled with strong coffee. They had never voted before and
most had no idea how long this was going to take. They would
not be hungry.

The ages of the women varied. There were the young and
the very old. Degrees of urbanity and formal education could
be found ranging from women who were backwoods elders
and barely literate to women with graduate and professional
degrees from fine universities. Their vocational and academic
standing had no bearing on their mission. They held one thing

in common: they were black and all their lives had been denied the most fundamental right of a citizen.

There was the clean fragrance of talcum powder in the air where the women stood, the kind rural people used to purchase from the Watkins or Rawleigh route salesmen who stopped at their doors each month. Also the subtle bouquet of Lily's pomade and germicidal soap. These melded with the lusty smell of slab bacon, hickory smoked and fried by first light on the low heat of wood-burning stoves. One woman, barely voting age at the time, remembers her grandmother standing with the group holding a faded, twelve-year-old copy of the Chicago *Tri-State Defender*. On it was the picture of the bloated and hideously disfigured body of Emmett Till lying in a casket with his grieving mother writhing in unspeakable grief. The fourteen-year-old lad had been murdered by two men, his body thrown into nearby Tallahatchie River, for allegedly flirting with a white woman storekeeper. The woman whose grandmother held the newspaper remembers that to her grandmother the picture was a grim reminder that she must do what she had come there to do. No matter the consequence. (Years later, I met the woman and her husband in a hotel restaurant and bar in Jackson. She said her grandmother died a few weeks after the election. She asked me not to use their names in a book. She didn't say why.)

A faint cantillating of the collective voices of the women

softened the clearing of throats and shuffling of feet of the men. There was a liturgical quality in the sounds but they were not recognizable as tunes. Not traditional spirituals nor familiar Delta blues. Perhaps they were instinctive African sounds or perhaps they were American originals unconsciously formed for this day and this occasion. In any case there was something reverent about the sounds, a sacred addendum to what was happening, the smells like incense in some ancient cathedral.

Neither group looked directly at the copper-skinned man moving past them. Instead they shot quick glances at a tall and thin Negro man who stood like a statue. He stood apart and seemed special. He wasn't watching the man moving down the aisle at all. His eyes moved methodically from side to side like the pendulum of a large clock, searching every area of the big room. Occasionally his eyes hesitated on one or another of the deputies. He seemed geared to exert himself if the need arose.

As the neatly dressed man advanced, a young white boy, no more than eight, exclaimed, "That's him. That's Robert Clark. He's the nigra what's running for office."

"What's a office?" a younger girl, perhaps the boy's sister, asked. They were milling around the front part of the store, near the checkout counter.

"I don't know," the boy said. "But I heard them talking at

church on Sunday. They said a nigra was running for office and if he won he would go to Jackson."

"I betcha he won't win," the girl said. "I betcha he won't ever see Jackson."

"Aw, you don't know," the boy said. "I heard all they said at church. And they said he might win. They said nigras are trying to take over on account of Lyndon Johnson."

"What's a lender johnny?" the girl asked, with an impish giggle.

"Aw, you don't know nothing. You're a silly goose."

"I do so know something." She was trying to keep her voice down now. "I can hear too. And I heard Mamma and Miss Fivash talking. They said this county won't put up with the government cramming the nigras down our throat."

"You young'uns best wait for the school bus outside," a white man said, an official poll attendant. "You can sit on the bench on the porch. So you won't get wet."

"I'll have to ask C. W.," the little girl said. "He told me to wait inside." She walked down the corridor formed by the two lines of men. She stopped in front of one of the men, a heavy-set, very dark man of about fifty. He bent over, picked her up and playfully threw her in the air. She giggled, louder than before, whispered in his ear, motioning to the man who had told them to leave. One of the deputies stood up briefly, watching, then sat down again.

The man she had called C. W. took off her rain hat, brushed her hair with his free hand, said something to her, lightly kissed her on the cheek, and put her down. Another example of that ineffable relationship that has existed between the races from slave days and still has not gone away. The care of their youngest, most impressionable little ones were entrusted to those they considered inferior, treacherous, unrefined. The little white girl held onto the black hand for a minute or so, then moved back to where the boy was waiting.

"He said stay inside," she said. "Away from the rain."

"That white man said best we wait outside," he answered.

"I can't help that," she said, looking toward the man.

"C. W. said wait in here and Mamma said always to mind C. W. so I'm staying in here."

"You better do what that white man said," the boy said.

"C. W. looks after me. Anyway, I ain't catching no school bus. Not til next year nohow. C. W.'s supposed to take me home."

"C. W.'s a nigra," the boy said, glancing around and trying to make sure no one could hear him.

"No such thing," she answered, edging away.

"Well, what is he then? If he ain't a nigra?"

"He's C. W. And that's all he is. He's C. W. and C. W. is my best friend in the whole world and I do what he says and he said wait in here so I'm staying in here like C. W. said do." The boy made no move to go outside on his own.

Robert Clark stopped at a table where a white man and two white women were seated. The two lines, lines of passion, moved gradually, silently but deliberately forward, forming a wide semicircle. Politically pauperized for so long, they seemed determined to miss nothing of this long-time-coming scene. The man with the tireless eyes remained in place, still searching. Still ready.

Robert Clark stopped in front of the woman at the end of the table. She had a jaded face, lily white with dull, gun-metal eyes. She wore a loose-fitting blouse with a high neck and a paisley shawl draped over her shoulders. The navy blue blouse had long sleeves with lace around the wrists, lace glistening like spider webs on damp fall mornings, leaving the fingers as the only bit of her pallid skin exposed to view.

A large gray clothbound ledger was on the table in front of the woman. She sighed nervously and seemed on the verge of weeping. A black man was about to invade her deep and uneasy space, a space which she earlier had assumed was for-ever. And was of God. She checked his name, sighed again, motioned him on.

The man at the end of the table, standing now, glared at Robert Clark as if giving him one last chance to change his mind about voting. Politics and voting had always been white folks' business in Holmes County. Wearing a faded tweed, once-green jacket with leather elbows and holding an unlighted straight-stemmed pipe between his teeth, the man might have been a proper Bostonian instead of a retired insurance adjustor in Ebenezer, Mississippi. He seemed strangely incongruous in the scene.

Robert Clark was calm. "I'm here to vote," he said, smiling and reaching out his hand as a bid for the paper ballot. After a long pause the man handed him a ballot and, without speaking, motioned with the pipe toward one of the voting booths.

Robert Clark knew that what he was doing was momentous, that it was not the first but was certainly another bold thrust toward justice. Slow in coming. An ineluctable moment everyone knew would come but which few whites acknowledged.

Robert Clark, teacher, coach, principal, bachelor, farmer, entered the booth and drew the curtain as casually as if it were the most routine thing. He soon reopened the curtain, stuffed the folded ballot into a locked wooden box, and walked back toward the door. The men opened a path, many of them nodding their heads approvingly as he passed. Then one by one they began making their way forward to join in this long delayed challenge of embedded wrongs.

As each man moved across the floor a woman from their group moved to join him. No one took the arm of her man as in a wedding procession or ceremonial, and they did not join hands. Just walked side by side across the wooden floor, the wide boards scuffed by many feet over the years. The procession moved deliberately and slowly toward the canvas-encased booths, each person requesting a ballot, each one entering what must have been to them a strange and mysterious realm. There was no hint of fear on the face of anyone. They would do what they had come there to do.

In less than a minute Robert Clark, at thirty-seven, a man with a baccalaureate degree from Jackson State College (by then Jackson State University) and a master's from Michigan State, a man who had taught high school and junior college for more than a dozen years, had voted for the first time in his life. And he had voted for himself. All the others, men and women, were voting for the first time also. They all voted for the same candidate.

As each couple cast their ballots and left the building the two deputies sat sulking by the door. Whatever they were thinking and feeling, they had made no move to stop what was taking place.

This is not the only chronicle of what happened that day in the village of Ebenezer. Another was written and published in the local newspaper. Titled "What Really Happened in Ebenezer Election Day, November 7, 1967," it gave a detailed account of willful interference in the voting process by young white men who claimed to be pollwatchers for black candidates. The writer was a precinct peace officer whose job was to protect the poll managers from interruptions or harrassment. He identified the white men as Paul Herbert Reiss of Attleboro, Massachusetts, a student at Harvard University Law

School, and Peter Haberfeld, an attorney from Carmel, California. At various times, according to the article, they were joined by local Negroes. Both men stated that they were there at the behest of the Mississippi Freedom Democratic Party. It is most likely that they had been recruited by the Student Nonviolent Coordinating Committee (SNCC) and assigned to the Mississippi Freedom Democratic Party by Lawrence Guyot, chairman of the MFDP.

The writer described various verbal threats that seemed a prelude to violence. One was detailed in this fashion:

He finally went outside and did not come back in until a Negro woman had come in to vote and had been refused because her name could not be found on any roles, County or Federal. Reiss rushed in and notified the manager that this woman "is going to be allowed to vote."

The manager asked him to go back to his seat and quit interfering with the election. He refused and kept refusing until my wife, an election clerk, said, "Something will have to be done with this man. I can not carry out my duties any longer with this man creating such a disturbance over my head."

I walked back to the shelf and picked up my pistol, which I had never worn before as an election peace officer, and put it in my pocket. I came around the corner and approached Reiss and said, "You will have to move back to your seat." He said,

"I am staying right here until this woman is voted." I asked him again and he replied the same.

I took him by the arm and said, "You are going back to your seat peacefully or otherwise." He repeated his reply.

Then I propelled him back to his seat; he missed the seat and sat on the floor. This was accidental.

The remaining several pages detailed further interruptions, some erupting into scuffles and fisticuffs. One was as follows: "The stranger said, 'You are not holding this election according to law. I am here to see that you do it according to law.'"

The account then described how Haberfeld was told that he was free to stay so long as he stood back and did not interfere with the process.

He turned to me and said, "I will stand anywhere in this building I want to stand. I will stand in front of this counter where you people are working, or, if I want to, I will come back behind the counter where the clerks and managers are."

I said to him, "To get back behind this counter, you will have to come over me." Then he said, "I will sit down on the bench with the other poll watchers and not cause any trouble."

But further trouble was reported in the precinct peace officer's account. One incident was a physical attack on a citizen the precinct peace officer had deputized on the spot. He had called the county sheriff for assistance after placing Haberfeld under arrest. The attack, by about a dozen or so young black men, occurred outside the building, and the precinct peace officer made what he described as a flying tackle upon the man he had deputized, thus throwing him out of the melee and into the street, allowing him to get away.

Another was a recounting of a group of young Negroes flinging the doors open with a loud crash and disrupting the vote counting. "They all rushed in like a charging football team. . . . I do mean strange because nobody there had ever seen any of them before. They were all dressed alike in some kind of dark clothing, suggesting that they belonged to some kind of society or group."

Robert Clark's recollection clarifies some of the confusion and ambiguities in the precinct peace officer's report. For example, he said the young men "rushed in like a charging football team." And that was what they were. Members of the high school football team. When it seemed no one from the public sector would be allowed to witness the counting of the votes as allowed by law, Mr. Clark, who was known by every black athlete in the county because of his coaching and refereeing of all sports, called Lexington and asked for some of the athletes to come to Ebenezer. These were young men, filled with determination and commitment garnered from recent federal legislation, some of them trained at the SNCC-sponsored freedom schools. The spirit of victory in realizing long-denied rights was in the air. The football players welcomed the chance to exert themselves in the cause. They were all dressed in black as the officer had described, because they wore gym pants and shirts.

In all probability the young pollwatchers did interfere with the process as it had been practiced in the past. They were young and determined, seasoned by the rhetoric of the movement activists who had overcome fear. The precinct peace officer addressed in his summary all those who raised questions about the procedure:

> . . . Communist agitators who came here from out of state; to all criminal agitators who came here from out of state; to all local agitators, criminal or foolish: You launched a horrible, vicious attack on what might have at first seemed to be a sleepy, defenseless little village. What you were actually doing was attacking a town inhabited by Red Blooded Americans who will fight for their homes. Why did you suddenly desist? Was it because nobody really likes death, when they are the ones who are going to die?

He continued:

> To my local white and colored friends I have this to say: In the midst of turmoil and strife it suddenly came to me that I had reached my last step backward. I will retreat before no

man who does not treat my family with courtesy and respect. If the people whose duty it is to protect our rights and punish the wrongdoer will not protect us we have no choice but to protect ourselves.

Robert Clark recalls the pollwatchers but not as knaves trying to destroy an election. Why would they want to destroy it? They were confident of victory unless there was duplicity in the tallying of votes. The pollwatchers for black candidates simply wanted some of the local citizens to observe the counting of ballots, which they understood to be their constitutional right. When they were refused, Robert Clark had a plan.

He had heard that a rumor was being spread around Ebenezer that there was "going to be some nigger blood shed that night." He called the FBI office and was told they were an investigative agency and could do nothing unless there was evidence of violation of a federal crime. Clark called the office of the Freedom Democratic Party in Lexington and asked that some of his football players be located and sent to Ebenezer, twelve miles away. About ten cars came. Robert Clark knew they were armed and he knew the whites present were armed. Except for those who rushed the vote counting area they simply milled around outside, doing nothing. Clark knew they were in a potentially explosive situation.

Outside the building a brouhaha had been mounting since the polls had closed. More and more whites assembled on the store porch and blacks continued to gather across the road in front of the voting place. The county sheriff, long known for his bad-tempered and sometimes brutal treatment of Negroes was, perhaps for the first time, frightened. He did what he had done in the past. "All right then. All of you are under arrest."

The Negro youngsters, in a mood approaching carnival, began jumping on the hood of the sheriff's car, packing the inside to capacity, and saying things like, "Yasuh, yasuh. Take us to duh jailhouse. We'se all under arrest. We'se ready to go to de capin's jailhouse." All in a spirit of jest, their words in mockery of stereotypical black dialect.

The sheriff, stymied for the first time in his handling of a situation involving Negroes, and seeing that there was no way he could transport all those he had placed under arrest, changed tactics. At first he said everyone would have to leave the grounds. Word had spread and still more people had gathered. Instead of everyone leaving, the crowd was growing and the threat of a shootout was mounting.

Several older men were present that night. Men who, not many years earlier, would not have dreamed of being allowed to vote. Mr. Eddie Hoover's old green truck door was latched with a rusty nail. When trouble seemed inevitable he removed the nail from the improvised latch, reached under the seat, and pulled out an old and very faded twelve-pound flour sack. Wrapped in the sack was a rusty .32 caliber pistol. Quickly canvassing the crowd he kissed the pistol, addressed it by his wife's name and said, "Annie, we have been married for more than fifty years. You have never let me down and I know you're not going to let me down tonight."

Although the sheriff was not accustomed to negotiating with Negro citizens, he was left with no choice. He suggested that he would let the Negroes leave a few at a time, thus, he reasoned, not depleting their ranks all at once. Burnwell Tate, speaking for the Negro group, said, "We ain't going nowhere." He said if one carload of whites would leave the premises, then a carload of blacks would leave. They would continue to alternate in that fashion until the yard was cleared and those inside could continue their work of counting the ballots.

The sheriff stood watching, pretending to direct the departing traffic, until the last carload was gone. What had promised to be the wholesale shedding of blood had been avoided.

A middle-aged black citizen, a respectable leader in the community now, told me that he had been one of the young students who had driven from Lexington to Ebenezer. He smiled as he talked about it. "What they didn't know was that a bunch of our boys had driven to the hills, doused the lights and for hours observed the going and coming below." He told me that another group drove in slow convoy fashion in and through Ebenezer until the vote counting was over.

"Would you have gone back down if the white folks had returned?" I asked.

His face turned serious. "I'm just glad it didn't happen that way," he said.

No one is certain of the exact sequence of events that damp November day. But one thing is certain. Before another sunrise, one who not long before would have been "boy" to many would be Mr. Robert George Clark, representative-elect of District Sixteen, Holmes and Yazoo counties, Mississippi. A lot of years, work, sacrifice, danger, and deaths had gone into making that day possible. A lot more would happen before Mr. Clark would go to Jackson.

But he would go.

II

I was in a somber mood the first time I met Robert George Clark. It was the fall of 1998. I had come from a weekend of activities at the Sixteenth Street Baptist Church in Birmingham where four little girls had died when a dynamite explosion ripped through the building shortly before the Sunday morning service. That was in 1963, four years before Robert Clark was even able to register to vote. Now, in 1998, I was meeting him for the first time. By then he had been in the Mississippi House of Representatives more than thirty years. Good years and bad.

It was a mild Sunday morning in Canton, Mississippi. By telephone we had agreed to meet there. I knew that Robert Clark was in the state legislature and had been for many years. I knew he was the first black citizen to be elected since Reconstruction. I had never seen him before but knew him immediately when he appeared outside a service station on the edge of town. With him was a beautiful tan-skinned woman wearing a Sunday-fashionable hat. Representative Clark had asked me to accompany him to a country church near Canton, the home church of Mrs. Clark.

I had not known that among other duties Mr. Clark was a Baptist preacher. It was the Thanksgiving Sunday service and he was to preach the sermon for the pastor. Before he began his sermon he asked me to bring greetings to the congregation. I had marveled at how like this setting was the Easter service described by William Faulkner in *The Sound and the Fury*, the occasion when Dilsey had brought the retarded Benjy Compson to church.

The children's choir, dressed in Sunday finery, had processed in, singing as they came. When I arose to greet the congregation my mind went back to the Sixteenth Street Baptist Church and the four young girls, the age and likeness of these children. I could not speak. I was somehow back to the day the church was bombed. My family and I were driving home from our church when we heard the news on the radio. Our oldest daughter had worn her first high heels that day and I had beamed at her loveliness when she came from her room in her organdy-trimmed blouse and skirt her mother had made, her little ankles like ropes challenging the new heels for balance. She was in the backseat with her ten-year-old sister. As we approached our house, it standing and safe, I supposed the Birmingham children were about the ages of our two girls. They had heard the news with us and were hushed of their merriment.

"Great God!" I said aloud. And then a silent expletive followed by a numbing thought. What if it were my little chil-

dren lying on marble slabs in a Birmingham morgue? Why was
the stash of explosives planted underneath the Sixteenth
Street Baptist Church? Why not underneath St. Philip's Episcopal Church where my family had just worshipped?

I knew the answer.

Concerning sins all of us white Christians minded to
receive the Holy Communion had prayed:

> The remembrance of them is grievous unto us;
> The burden of them is intolerable.

Grievous? Intolerable? Really? The words had seemed perfunctory. Droning on behind the priest. "We do earnestly
repent, and are heartily sorry for these our misdeeds." How
many of us would share the anguish of those Birmingham
mothers? How many would find the dynamite blast an intolerable burden? It would be for a young Birmingham lawyer
named Charles Morgan to stand before his civic club and pro-
claim that every last white person in the city and state was
guilty of the horrendous crime of killing children at prayer.

As for us, next Sunday we would again hear the words of
the priest: "Ye who do truly and earnestly repent you of your
sins, and are in love and charity with your neighbours, and
intend to lead a new life. . . ." And again we would all kneel at
the altar. And lie. Now I recall being tormented by that line of
thought and of not going to communion for a long time.

Those hurried and random recollections raced through my mind as I stood before a black congregation in my native state with a lump in my throat that would not let me speak. Finally I was able to say that my cup was running over because of the experience of the day before when I revisited the place where children had been sacrificed on the altar of bigotry. Children who were the same as these dressed-up children standing now for their choral offering.

I was aware that all eyes were fixed on me. An alien quiet had swept the congregation. At first, sensitive to the very whiteness of my skin, I thought it was a judgmental quiet, the stares hostile. Then suddenly, as even the quiet intensified, I realized that it was a moment of grace, that the black congregation was crying with me and that together we were weeping tears of reconciliation.

My white self does not have to bear this burden alone.

Robert Clark, standing on the dais wearing his flowing clerical robe, spread his arms in a moment of expiation and I was able to continue my account of the previous day's experience.

Representative Clark, as preacher now, turned to the youthful singers and said that the lesson to be learned was that not all white people were their enemies.

After the service we ate dinner in the downstairs area. Turkey, ham, pork chops, dressing, fried chicken, turnip greens, cornbread, crowder peas, salads, sauces, cakes, pies. We drank sweet tea.

A sacrament?

Have mercy upon you; pardon and deliver you from all your sins; confirm and strengthen you in all goodness.

Maybe it is true. Maybe it really is true and is happening here.

Robert George was not the first Clark of color to be involved in Mississippi politics. His grandfather had been chairman of the Hinds County Republican Party. That, however, had been in 1875, almost a hundred years earlier.

With the end of the Civil War, politics in Mississippi was a melange, a mortar stirred by a thousand pestles. Confusion prevailed. Freed slaves, some motivated by the most noble of virtues, others propelled by the same primordial hubris that plagues us all, strived to throw off the vestiges of enslavement by gaining ascendancy in the political process. In league with the carpetbaggers (northerners who came south for personal economic and political reasons) and the scalawags (antebellum southerners who were active Republicans), the former slaves were a factor to be reckoned with in everything political. And just as often they were pawns in that process. One such occasion was when Governor Adelbert Ames, Republican governor in 1875, was reported to have said that the blood of a few Negroes would force President Grant to send federal troops and guarantee that the Republican Party would remain in power. It was in this atmosphere that rioting broke out in several towns and cities. A major one took place in the fall of 1875 in Clinton, fifteen miles west of the capital city of Jackson. A huge Republican rally with free barbecue was planned for September 4, and Democrats were invited to attend and speak. When gunfire was heard during one of the speeches (according to the best account, it came from a small group of drunken white youths), a riot erupted in which several people from both races were killed. Rumors that the most unconscionable atrocities had been inflicted by blacks upon innocent whites circulated as far west as Vicksburg and as far east as Jackson. By nightfall a special train brought armed men from Vicksburg and other communities along the way. For two days there were random assaults upon blacks. Between twenty and thirty were killed. Bummers from the Negro sections were said to have retaliated at night. But not on the same scale.

Not many days later two men from the vicinity of Clinton, William Clark, a former slave, and Jesse Furver, a white yeoman farmer, were talking just outside William Clark's cypress-shingled dogtrot cabin where he lived alone. No one now knows exactly what they were saying. Nor the precise accent and elocution. No effort is made here to duplicate either.

Jesse Furver was sitting on a fidgety sorrel mare. William Clark was leaning casually against a spreading catalpa tree which provided shade in summer and also fishing worms, which both men had picked often from the leaves as bait for the lengthy lamper eels, hefty buffalo, and bluecats that populated the dark waters of the Big Black River.

The two men had been close. As close as white and black could comfortably be in 1875. Jesse Furver was older than William Clark. He had moved to Hinds County from Holmes County around 1840, not long after the Choctaw removal to the West. He had been sympathizing and friendly toward the Choctaws, especially a young Choctaw boy his age. He had not wanted to remain on the farm his father had settled after the Treaty of Dancing Rabbit Creek and as soon as he was of age he moved near Clinton where he at first worked, then bought, a portion of a war- wracked plantation. It was near the plantation on which William Clark was a slave at emancipation.

Clark was young to hold such an important position as leader in the Republican Party, but black leadership following emancipation did not depend on longevity.

The two had a private fishing hole at a horseshoe bend in the river near Bovina, a bend that slowed the current, giving it a brief rest before it hurried on to the Mississippi, that ravenous old man that claimed ascendancy from Minnesota to the Gulf of Mexico. The impeded flow of the current provided an ideal spot for the fish to spawn in hollow logs and cypress brush.

The two men spoke in a calm and friendly manner. They were discussing the terrible drought and heat that had plagued Mississippi all summer. It had left grown trees dead, cattle dying from dried-up watering ponds and lack of grazing, newborn calves with heat strokes, newly farrowed pigs dead at the sow's paps. The summer had been a medley of disaster.

Suddenly Jesse Furver dismounted, tied the bridle rein to a low-hanging limb and faced William squarely. His bearing was completely changed. Where he had been calm and friendly before, now his face was flushed and there was a decided tremor in his hands and his voice rose to a high pitch.

"You've had your last chance, William. I have to kill you tonight." William Clark knew that Furver was active in the organized effort to regain political control from Black Republicans. He knew that, as a leader of the Hinds County Republican Party, he was a target. He had had several visitations before the Clinton riots, men ordering him with vituperative language to leave the county, but no one had threatened to kill him. Certainly not his old fishing buddy Jesse Furver. Some Negro leaders in the Republican Party had been intimidated into leaving. Some had gone voluntarily to Natchez, New Orleans, or Memphis and more than a few had been killed.

"Why are you talking like this, Mr. Jess?"

"You know why, William. We've tried to get you to leave

for months now and you won't go. I hate to do it. But I owe it to my family, to my people, my race. Your people are damaging and destroying everything. Everything. Civilization. Our rights. Our heritage. Just everything. White people have rights too. The scalawags and carpetbaggers are killing us and you're helping." He was almost shouting now, staccato, flailing his arms and moving slowly away from William Clark. "We've had our meeting. We cast lots and I was the one chosen." There was a long pause as he studied his own sun-tanned and calloused hands. Hands that, he was saying, would shortly hold the instrument of death. "Fact is, I volunteered," he went on. "So now I have to do it as soon as the sun goes down."

Clark showed no fear. He seemed possessed of, or by, some pristine power that removed him from any threat of bodily harm. Any reality of death appeared impossible. He moved as Furver moved, talking as he did. He humbly explained that he meant no harm to Mr. Jess, to the white folks, to anyone. He acknowledged that he was an officer in the Hinds County Republican Party, had been elected to the office by his people. But he was also a minister to his people, was trying to lift them up as best he could. He had helped organize the first General Baptist Convention, and had organized and pastored the Pleasant Green Baptist Church, then serving Clinton and Bolton. He could read and write and was teaching others.

Furver did not respond to anything Clark told him. Instead he remounted and reined his horse around. "I'll be back."

William Clark moved in front of the mare and seized the reins. "Don't go just yet, Mr. Jess," he pleaded. "I got to tell you something."

Without moving from where he stood, he began to talk about the hardships he had known since he was taken from his mother and sent from Alabama to Mississippi. He talked of the slave children being kept in a pen all day, fed milk and cornbread from a trough like pigs. Ate with their hands. "You were old enough to remember, Mr. Jess. How I never had a pair of shoes, summer or winter, until after slavery and how I wore a little cotton dress and nothing else." Jesse had given William his first shoes. Secondhand.

"But why wouldn't you leave? We gave you chances, warnings, and you wouldn't go. Now it's too late."

Clark tried to explain that to leave would be a betrayal of his people. He was their leader. He was of them. Jesse did not answer.

Like monks at prayer a gathering of mosquitoes knelt on William's arms, sinking their greedy needles to drink of his now endangered blood. Suddenly Clark began to talk Bible talk. He was not preaching in the shouting, singsong fashion of many black preachers of the day. More in a lecture style, like he might do in Sunday school to young children. He talked of Cain and Abel. Brother killing brother. For what? For power. There would be a price. Offsprings Jubal, Jabal, and Tubal-Cain. Names from Genesis. Names from Freemasonry. Jesse recognized the names. Sons of Lamech, of the line of

Cain. Killed a mere lad to avenge a piddling bruise. Methuselah. Nine hundred and sixty-nine years old but did nothing. Nothing except polluting and poisoning, never cleansing and purifying. Still and yet, he had a grandson named Noah, second father of mankind.

Even the most baneful could be used by the Almighty.

Jesse Furver sat on his horse, gazing into the distance, pretending not to listen. But listening. Listening to a remarkable recitation of biblical stories and characters, good and evil. A recitation Jesse intuited had something to do with what was happening at that very moment.

William went on. From Aaron, eloquent of tongue, who could speak when Moses could not, but who built an idol, a calf of gold, and explained it with silliness.

Even the most righteous could do evil things.

On to Zephaniah who declared that God was the ruler of all nations, all races, all peoples, but demanded righteousness of everyone.

Don't assume you are special.

Then to Onesimus, a slave who ran away but returned to Philemon. As brother.

There was a long silence, neither man moving. Then William Clark began his homily again with the story of Jonathan and David, two men who loved each other. Instead of one taking the life of the other, one gave his own life to save the life of the other. Dropping the reins and looking intently into the face of Jesse, who sat on his steed in feigned indifference, William quoted, still from Genesis, still by rote, now with resignation: "I am distressed for thee, my brother Jonathan: very pleasant hast thou been unto me: thy love to me was wonderful, passing the love of women. How are the mighty fallen, and the weapons of war perished."

I love you. The once mighty Confederacy is no more, and all the vast weapons are of no account.

Some would have been astounded at the eloquence of someone ten years from being owned. But Jesse Furver knew he was facing a man of exceptional intellect, unusually accomplished in logic and elocution.

"I have to kill you, William," Jesse Furver said again.

"Let someone else do it, Jesse," William Clark said. He said it like a father giving advice to a son. He had not responded in an obsequious fashion throughout the conversation. Nor did he now. Without another word he turned and walked inside. Jesse Furver rode away.

Reverend Clark knew that he would not run. He was

dispirited at the thought that these were his last hours on earth, but he had an abiding faith in a sovereign God who would, after all, have the last word. It did not disturb him that he had learned of that God in a state of bondage. He knew that his people had been on this continent for at least two centuries, longer than most of those who presumed to own them. So he claimed the land as his own. In addition, he thought of the father he never knew who loved him in the womb. His blood mother was a slave woman in Alabama. The man she loved but could not marry was a Creek Indian. His people had been here long before either black or white were on the scene. Before William had been taken from his mother she had told him the story. Her lover had come to her quarters just before daybreak, awakened her, held her close and said that he would never see her again. The infamous Treaty of Washington, signed in 1832, had accomplished most of its demonic intent. The plenary mischief of the European whites had included removal of most Creeks to the West, leaving some as nomads surviving in swamps and fields and some as slaves in Alabama. William Clark's Creek father might have been from the latter group. Perhaps he was being sold to another plantation, returned to a stockade from which he had escaped, or was caught in one of the periodic dragnets that had escaped the earlier removals to Oklahoma. Whatever the case, William Clark never saw his father.

Inside his cabin he removed the small Bible from its stand

beside his shuck-mattress bed. Without opening it he recited from the Eighty-second Psalm. "But ye shall die like men, and fall like one of the princes." He opened the book and read silently the Seventy-ninth Psalm, except part of the eleventh verse which he spoke aloud: ". . . according to the greatness of thy power preserve thou those that are appointed to die."

When Jesse returned in less than an hour, the sun had gone down but there was still a whisper of light. William Clark met him at the door. Jesse was calm again. William invited him inside and offered him water from a stone pitcher. Jesse began explaining his plan. His wording was as if they were discussing the most ordinary matter and none of it had been discussed earlier. He would march William to a clearing on the edge of the swamp. There would be other men there, perhaps a dozen, all dressed in white robes and headdress. (Four years earlier a federal law had been passed, the Ku Klux Klan Act, making night riding, violent behavior, a violation of federal statute. That law, however, had not destroyed the Klan.) The men would say nothing and no one would follow them as they marched on into the deep jungle-like woods. He explained that when one was elected for a number three, the code words for assassination, he had to do it without accompaniment. That way there was never a witness to testify against a fellow Klansman.

Jesse explained that when the two of them were far enough away, the other men would hear two loud salvos. "I will go back to the station, the Klud (Klan chaplain) will conduct the Ceremony of Accomplishment and we will all go home. Any member who ever talks, no matter what the circumstances, will be killed."

"Don't you do it, Jesse," William begged again. "Let someone other than you do it. Someone I don't know."

"This is the plan," Jesse went on. Still as if nothing else had been said earlier. "My rifle here is a Sharps Repeater." The Sharps Repeater had been designed a few years earlier and was for long distances and accuracy. It could also be heard for a long way. "There will be no mistaking when I have fired."

Jesse stepped outside and looked in all directions. Back inside he lowered his voice and continued. "The two shots the men will hear will be fired over your head. You will fall to the ground crawling. Crawling fast. Crawling like a spreading adder. When you have crawled far enough, you will get up. Get up running. Running like a deer. Running through the swamp. Fording the Big Black. Running again. All the way to Vicksburg. No one will look for you in the briars and dense underbrush and trees. Coyotes and bears and wild dogs devour bodies in no time out there. When there is new blood. Your people will not look for you for they will know they won't find you."

Neither man spoke now. Not until Jesse Furver said, "But you must swear. Swear on your Bible there that you will never, ever be seen in Hinds County again. Go ahead. Put your hand on the Bible there."

"You know I don't swear, Mr. Jess." He had gone back to the more formal way of addressing Furver. "I just can't do no swearing. The book there says don't swear."

Jesse was furious. He moved closer to William, speaking in the same staccato way as before. "No! No! No! You, by god, won't swear. But you would kill. Kill me."

"Oh, no sir, Mr. Jess. I wouldn't ever kill you. You know I wouldn't ever kill nobody. The book says don't kill."

"Can't you understand, William?" Jesse was trying to corner his anger. "If I shoot over your head and then you're seen in this county again, ever, then they'll, by god, kill me. I would have betrayed my people. And it would be your fault. My blood would be on your hands as much as theirs. And the betraying too. You say you can't betray your people. All right. But you can betray me. And kill me as well. Don't you understand? Don't you see!? Don't you see!!?"

William Clark stood thinking. He rubbed his temples. Rubbed his eyes. He did understand. Did see. And at that moment he knew what he must do. He moved to face Jesse. He extended his hand. "I won't ever come back, Jesse." It was solemn oath enough.

"Then let's go," Jesse said.

They had moved outside as they talked. William stood fixed upon the ground. The good earth. His mother's people had known and had been dragged from the earth, the land, the ground of West Africa. Earth they knew and loved. His father's people had been defrauded of and removed from land called Creek, earth they knew and loved as much as the West Africans. Where William Clark was standing was the only bit of the earth he had ever known. Life on it had not been easy. But it was not the doings of the land. He knew that now. Until that moment he had not realized that he actually loved this ground. The earth where he stood. Even the nearby plot where he and the other slave children had been fenced in and fed like young shoats. He had heard the stories of how his long-ago ancestors scooped up and ate handsful of dirt so that they might take something of their past, their land into captivity. Now he felt a craving to take with him a bit of earth where he had learned and loved and worked.

"I reckon your folks would be suspicious if I put a little something in a poke," he said, stooping to pick up a bit of dirt.

"Let's go," Jesse said again.

Clutching the dirt in his hand William turned and looked back at his tiny house, and on beyond it at the meager dwellings of the others. He saw smoke curling from wood stoves where women were cooking supper after a long day in the fields. Children were playing on hard-packed dirt yards, frolicking in the last light of day. Someone was singing. And in the distance he imagined he could hear the call of the cast-iron bell at Pleasant Green Baptist Church, beckoning the flock to the midweek service where Reverend Clark would read the Bible and pray and teach them a little more writing.

"Let's go," Jesse repeated. Wiliam took one more fleeting yet all-encompassing glance, dropped the dirt, and began walking toward the dark woods.

III

Not all was as quiet around the Sixteenth District on the first Tuesday in November 1967 as things had been in the Ebenezer store on that election morning. More like what happened there in the afternoon and evening. Many could simply drive to the polls, cast their ballots, and leave. Plantation workers and day laborers found it more difficult. In late fall planters would pool their equipment and "croppers" and move them from place to place. Near Tchula a plantation overseer approached a convoy of mechanical cotton pickers moving into place to prepare for the day's picking. Out of the smoky dawn, even before he reached the lead driver, he began to recite a list of instructions of what had to be done that day. A fretting wind blowing across the Delta was bringing the rain that was already falling in Ebenezer ever closer. Rain prayed for in the savage heat of July but now threatening carnage to the Delta's lifeline. It was vital that the cotton be picked and sheltered while still dry.

"Here's a list of things got to be done today," the overseer told the driver. "Get the machines all fueled, check the oil and water, move the pickers to the west side of the field and space the pickers. Make sure everyone has their water jugs on the machine. We need this field done by dinnertime. Then we'll move on to the one across the road and finish it by suppertime. When your women bring your dinner, you can eat while you drive. Don't waste time. Got to beat the rain."

The driver idled the engine and spoke to the boss man. His tone was polite but his words were heard by the white man as uncharacteristically insolent.

"Yessir. We'll get it all done. Soon as I get back. I got to go vote first. Won't take long."

They were words from a field hand never before heard by the plantation boss. "Vote! Vote?! What the hell you talking about, boy. We don't have time for such bullshit."

"Yessir, I know we need to get the cotton in ahead of the rains. But this is the day. Only day to vote. Tomorrow be too late."

The white man's face flushed red, veins standing out on his neck like mole runs. "You know what you're saying, boy? Know who you talking to? Now let's get moving. Don't have all day."

"I don't mean to 'spute your word, Boss, but I got to go vote. Promised Coach Clark I'd be there."

"Vote. Vote?" the man screamed. "All right, go vote. But get your ass off the place. Gimme them keys. I won't be needing you no more. Go on. Go on. But don't come back. Gimme them keys."

For a century those had been the only words necessary. The black man would have had no choice. He would go back to work. Not on this day. Instead he calmly handed over the keys and started to walk away. He glanced over his shoulder at the big machines and the acres of bursting lily-white bolls stretching as far as he could see. He stopped and turned around, like saying good-bye to old friends. The cotton as well as the men. This was the only life he had ever known. Cotton. What would he do? What of his wife, his children, his aged mother who was in his care?

Pausing, he saw the overseer, who seemed pleased now. The keys were the metaphor for power. And he had them in his hand. But keys are of no value unless they are unlocking something. The boss man turned to hand the keys to someone else. A substitute tractor driver or truck driver. Instead what he saw when he turned was a dozen or so other men. They had all dismounted from the high cabs of cottonpickers and bean combines, off tractor seats or from inside one or another of the big trucks. They already knew what they were going to do. Each man stood with keys in his hand. Standing as they had never stood before. Standing as a barnyard choir of cocks auguring change. It was not a new song they were singing. For hundreds of years they had sung it. They knew the words. Now they were beginning to put words and tune together. They had had new teachers, "outsiders" who stood as insiders. Singing. Marching. Exhorting. All about keys. Keys releasing

pristine power that had been held in check but was now exert-
ing itself and would never again lie dormant.

They had heard the song as sung by Mrs. Fannie Lou
Hamer, a stocky, raven-skinned woman from nearby Sun-
flower County. Mrs. Hamer, with an artesian manner and
enormous courage, knew both the words and the tune. She
sang of how she had started picking cotton at six, of how the
overseer bet her a piece of candy she couldn't finish an entire
row, of how seductive had been the thought of sweet licks of
peppermint sticks, but of how, even at her tender age, she felt
violated as she ate the prize. She was the last of twenty children. So she sang to and of the children and of how she could
never have little ones of her own because the plantation
owner had had her sterilized against her knowledge while she
was in the hospital for another ailment.

"Is this America? Is this America?" she had chanted at the
Democratic National Committee in Atlantic City in 1964 as
she opened her heart with all the pain of the years: cheated at
sharecropping, a beating in Winona jail that left her permanently injured, being denied personhood. She had traversed
the Delta and the nation singing her songs, delivering her
prophetic orations on the sins of the nation against people of
color. She told of how she had attended a meeting in her tiny
church in Ruleville being addressed by one of the "outsiders"
become insiders. Reverend James Bevel.

Bevel had grown up in nearby Itta Bena. Yet his revolutionary ideas made him an outsider. "Outsider" had to do with ideology, not proximity. He was no stranger to the spirit of white supremacy. He had dropped out of American Baptist Seminary in Nashville, where he had been a leader in the first sit-in movement in 1960. When he returned to the Delta as a field secretary for the Student Nonviolent Coordinating Committee, many of his neighbors thought him crazy. He agreed, saying that creative insanity was necessary to challenge segregation in Mississippi. He talked in the little Ruleville church of starting citizenship schools, of organizing boycotts, marches, and protests, and especially of encouraging black citizens to register to vote, that right they had long been denied. When the young preacher asked, in the manner of an altar call in a summer revival, for volunteers to go to the courthouse to register, Mrs. Hamer, without hesitation and without considering the consequences, raised her hand. Reverend Bevel had aroused the congregation to an apostolic fervor, preaching from Matthew 16:3, on the generations who "discern the signs of the times." Generally the invitation at the close of such a sermon was for those who would volunteer their lives to "full-time Christian service." It was called "surrendering to preach." Bevel's invitation was for volunteers to go the next day to the courthouse and register to vote. Fannie Lou Hamer had heard the call and was surrendering.

Denied the right to register the next day, the volunteers were stopped by a policeman as they journeyed home. It was part of the concerted program of intimidation by white officials. While the officer interrogated the volunteer driver of their bus, Mrs. Hamer sang to the frightened souls, calming them in their feeling of terror.

When they had watched her on television from Atlantic City, men and women had cheered, "That's our lady." (So convincing had been Mrs. Hamer's message on the convention floor that President Lyndon Johnson had hurriedly called a press conference to get her off the national television coverage.) Now, some of the same men stood with their most powerful weapons in their hands—keys to stilled vehicles of harvest.

"We have to go vote, too," one of the men said, starting to hand over the keys he held.

The overseer was dumbfounded by what he was hearing. He had heard the stories of the outsiders who had come to Mississippi to "stir up trouble." He actually believed what he had been told all his life: "Our colored people are the happiest people in the world if others would only leave them alone." But those young apostles of equity would no longer "leave them alone." They had come to preach deliverance to the captives of segregation and rampant racism.

The men with the keys had other keys they had not realized before. Keys which had been there all along and which the "outsiders" who flocked to Mississippi in the early and middle sixties confirmed and identified. The plantation overseer did not know of their potency; did not know that these young people had come with promises, promises quickly banked by souls long hungry for surcease from ancient wrongs, people whose ascendants had come to this bluff and fertile gorge as chattel of encroachers who possessed the land by duplicity and kept it by a system it would take a barbarous war to end. He still thrived on the notion that his "croppers" were happy and content with this system that had replaced the old system of slavery but which in many ways was no different.

He knew nothing of the real history of the Student Nonviolent Coordinating Committee, of its origin on Easter Sunday of 1960 in Raleigh, North Carolina, where several hundred Negro students convened and, under the wise counsel of an extraordinary woman named Ella Baker, formed an organization that would, by remarkable bravery, sacrifice, and steadfastness, change the nation. He didn't know of the brilliance and tenacity of a courtly young New Yorker named Bob Moses who chose the most forbidding places like Greenwood and McComb where he would be beaten and jailed in a fashion unthinkable in a civilized society. Chuck McDew, John Lewis, Bernard Lafayette, James Bevel, Lawrence Guyot, Ed Brown— the list was long of young men who faced death to teach of the keys to freedom.

Or of the strength and influence of the women who came or were already in place. Beautiful Diane Nash, who in

Nashville led a line of twenty-five hundred marchers to face the mayor and ask him directly if he thought it was right for department and variety stores to sell black customers anything in the store except a seat at the lunch counter, not relaxing her grip on his conscience until he acknowledged that she and her troops were right. Diane Nash, that picture of midwestern urbanity, who had come south with only education in mind but who stayed to marry Mississippian James Bevel and would have had their first child in a Mississippi jail rather than be bailed out for a bogus charge but the local court would not have it and so released her.

And local women too. Victoria Adams of Hattiesburg, Unita Blackwell in Mayersville, Annie Devine of Canton—black Mississippi women who opened their homes and hearts to the young students and nurtured and protected them as best they could. In return, the students, these "outsiders," fought for their freedom, even with their lives.

Standing there on a damp Delta November morning, the man facing the field hands had apparently already forgotten the freedom vote in 1963 when ninety-three thousand black citizens who had been turned away from legal registration turned out in a mock election to vote for Aaron Henry, a black pharmacist from nearby Clarksdale, for governor. And for a white Methodist preacher named Ed King for lieutenant governor. Although their votes counted for nought in the actual race for the two offices, they disproved forever the white Citizens' Council's propaganda that Negroes really didn't care about voting. The success of the mock election inspired the young students to conceive of an entire summer devoted to organizing a political party.

In Holmes County the men standing with the keys had heard of Chaney, Goodman, and Schwerner, killed in Neshoba County, whose deaths only encouraged hundreds of students to flock to the state for what they called Mississippi Freedom Summer. Those who came were mainly white; black bodies made little impression on the prevailing power structure.

SNCC, and Dr. King's Southern Christian Leadership Conference, and the martyred Medgar Evers's beloved NAACP, and the Congress of Racial Equality (CORE) all worked together, sometimes with conflict, under the umbrella of something they called COFO, the Council of Federated Organizations, but it was the young who provided the energy, the excitement, the poetry. In places like Holly Springs, Gluckstadt, Harmony, and Palmer's Crossing they set up freedom schools to prepare young and old to register to vote. On this day their efforts were bearing fruit.

On the other side of the county, rain was falling and Robert Clark was casting his ballot for a seat in the Mississippi state legislature. On this side, a dozen or so men stood challenging the entire electoral system. The overseer knew what they were saying. "You let us go vote or this cotton will rot in the fields."

The challenge had come before. It had come in Atlantic City when Mrs. Hamer and the Freedom Democratic Party had stood before America and said it was they, not the "regulars," the all-white delegation, who should be seated. There they met with minimal success. This predestined Tuesday in November would be different.

As the white overseer, the one formerly with unlimited power, stood there, maybe he was pondering what the owner of the land would do in the situation. That man lived in Memphis. No time for that. In any case he would not risk telling the landlord that a situation had arisen which his overseer couldn't handle. He was as vulnerable as the field hands. He could follow his glands of bigotry and lose a crop and maybe his job or he could use his head and try to bluff his way out of the dilemma. For that dumfounded moment perhaps he realized that he was as much a victim of the system as the black men who stood offering their keys and their livelihood in exchange for exercising a right white citizens took for granted. For that fleeting trice, maybe he knew in his Mississippi bones that they were all victims of the seeds of time, seeds neither he nor they had planted but whose harvest was now beginning, a harvest the outcome of which he could not yet imagine.

Holmes County was an enigma to white Mississippians. When the civil rights movement came to Holmes, it was not rejected amd mistrusted by local black citizens the way it was in many areas. Certainly the power structure was all white and had been white since Reconstruction, but there was a difference here. In most counties in the state the school calendars for black children were determined by the cotton season. In the spring there would be no school so that black children could "chop cotton" or cut sassafras or persimmon sprouts alongside their parents. In the fall schools would close to allow for picking the cotton. Not so in Holmes County. Although whites had recovered most of the land lost after the Civil War, there was still a great deal of ownership by blacks, land such as the sizeable acreage Robert Clark's great-grandfather had bought for a dollar an acre after freedom, land that the Holmes County folk would defend with arms when attacked later by racist antagonists.

The people in this county among whom Robert Clark had grown up were used to helping each other. With labor and tools. It was this history of collective support that undergirded the struggle for freedom there. When Holmes County entered the movement, its work was dominated by men, unlike almost every other area of the struggle where women were first to step forward. Men in other areas were more easily intimidated than women. There was more of a frontier spirit among the men of Holmes County. The passive, nonviolent resistance preached by Dr. King in other areas never gained much support here. The men were rural, and guns were as customary in the homes for protection against burglary and for shooting game for food as the Big Ben clocks were for marking the hours. Fact is, when Robert Clark was eleven years old, his father, a gentle man by frontier standards, shot and killed a man who was attempting to break into his home. When the high sheriff came to take the father to jail, for reasons Robert Clark has never understood, he took the boy to jail also. Young Robert was in jail along with his father and a brother who had been arrested too. In keeping with the frontier notion of justice, even under a racist system, a white aristocratic lawyer named Neilson successfully defended the father on the ground that protecting one's family from an intruder was not a crime. In the heat of passion during the turbulent sixties that notion was not espoused among Holmes County whites. The proverb "A man's home is his castle" did prevail in Holmes County in the 1960s among black citizens but not whites. For example, when Hartman Turnbow's house was fired upon as reprisal for his being the first Negro in the county to register to vote, he was quickly arrested and charged with firing into his own house. Mr. Turnbow was undaunted. He became one of the county's most effective civil rights activists.

Women participated in the movement in Holmes but it was the men who led the way. Hearing of the intense activity of the movement in nearby Greenwood, a group of Holmes County men went there and asked the young activists to send SNCC field secretaries to help them. Other communities, fearing reprisal from local whites, had sought to dissuade the young revolutionaries.

All the engines were quiet now. As were the men who stood considering the one who for years had controlled their destiny. The only sound they could hear now was his angry, bull-like breathing. And the rhythmic jingle of the keys each man held ready to present to the overseer, a solemn oblation.

He stood studying the dark clouds slowly moving over the loess bluffs toward the Delta. He fished a cigarette from the heavily starched denim shirt. He patted both front pockets of the gray Duckhead trousers but found no lighter. The man who had been given the day's work schedule and who, a few minutes earlier, had surrended his keys and started to walk away, moved forward, struck a wooden kitchen match with his thumbnail, cupped his hands to protect the flame from the wind.

"Thank you, Lonnie," the overseer said. Sincerely. As if no feathers had been ruffled. He took a deep drag from the unfiltered cigarette, held the smoke in his lungs as long as he could, exhaled in short spurts. The other men stood motionless. Watching. There was an occasional flicker from one or another of the keys as the sun risked a peek from behind the gathering clouds. Like a cheerleader.

The overseer moved one step closer. "Well, all right then," he said. In a soft timbre. He feigned a laugh. "Everybody on the back of the pickup. I'll take all of you. Might as well go on and vote myself. But we do have to hurry. Lonnie, you get up front."

"Thank you, sir," Lonnie answered. "We appreciate it but we have to take our womenfolks. They have to go vote too."

Count thirty-four votes for Robert G. Clark. All still in the house but now with the key. History becoming archival.

Bob Dylan had been right. The times they were a-changin'.

"And that was your grandmother on your mother's side?" I asked.

"No. My great-grandmother. My granddaddy Jones's mother."

I was talking, mostly listening, to Mr. Robert George Clark, member of the Mississippi House of Representatives, as he wrestled an aging Ford sedan off an access road and onto Interstate 55, heading north. We had just stopped at one of Jackson's most colorful and prestigious "meat and three" restaurants. Fine barbeque too. As Mr. Clark was paying the cashier, another woman was taking a box of big beef bones to his car. "For my dogs," he told me. "Hunting dogs?" "Uh, huh. Hunting dogs. Fox and coons. Hunt deer too, but not with dogs. Dogs love those bones. Take them a box every week. They save the bones after the barbeque is pulled off. Always a little left for gnawing." We were on our way to Holmes County, his homeplace. I would soon learn that it had also been the homeplace of his parents, two sets of grandparents, and one set of great-grandparents. "And that happened in Alabama?" I asked.

"Uh, huh. Alabama. I'm not able to tell you exactly what part of Alabama. I think, though, that it was somewhere in what they call the Black Belt. Somewhere around the Black Warrior River. What is now Greene County."

He gained speed as we moved along the flat and straight highway, carefully observing the speed limit and letting impatiently careless drivers have whatever of the road they wanted. Running parallel to the highway was the Illinois Central Railroad with its panting diesel engines pulling scores of flatcars and boxcars loaded with pulpwood, river gravel, and an assortment of heavy equipment, heading for ports along the Mississippi River and Gulf Coast. They sometimes drowned the sound of our voices. The car had no air-conditioning and the Mississippi air blew hot against my cheek as I turned toward him, trying to miss nothing he said above the sounds outside.

"Greene County," I repeated. Not as a question. "That was a tough county for the young civil rights workers in the 1960s." He smiled knowingly, said nothing.

"I read where they've reinstated chain gangs in Alabama," I said, trying to draw him out on the subject of civil rights.

"New Bedford, Massachusetts, too," he chuckled. "Bristol

County, Massachusetts. I lived there for a year. Didn't see a lot of difference between there and here, just to tell you the truth."

I moved back to his great-granddaddy. He talked methodically but ceremoniously, like it was part of a formal lecture.

"My great-granddaddy was born early one morning," he began again. "Later that morning the mistress of the plantation came over to the slave quarters. Came right to my great-great-grandma's cabin. 'Rachel, let me see your baby,' she said, turning the little bunting back without waiting for permission. She didn't comment on the baby. Instead she said something like, 'Rachel, I know you're awful tired. I'm going to send you your supper.'"

The representative of the forty-seventh district to the Mississippi legislature fell silent. Like it was my turn to say something or ask a question. When I didn't and after a long pause he said, "Next morning Grandma Rachel was dead."

I thought I understood what he was telling me but wasn't sure. "Poisoned?"

"Poisoned. Uh, huh. She knew that the slave's baby was her husband's baby too. And she wasn't going to have it."

"Was she trying to kill the baby too?" I asked, not sure whether a mother's first milk would pass on the poison. He explained that he didn't know about all that but he didn't think so. After all, the baby was chattel and could be sold. He speculated that they probably put the baby on sugar water and then a wet nurse, which most large plantations had to suckle newborn babies so the mother could return to the fields.

And that was what happened. He was sold. To a plantation in Mississippi. The Jones plantation. Mississippi had been admitted as a state in 1817, but until 1830 and the signing of the Treaty of Dancing Rabbit Creek, large tracts still belonged to the Choctaw nation. Holmes County, where Ebenezer is located, was not formed as a geographical entity until 1833, and it was probably about that time that the great-grandfather of Representative Robert Clark was sold as a child to the Jones plantation.

Apparently the Alabama planter felt some degree of fondness or responsibility for the lad and asked the new owner not to assign him to the hard life of a field hand. Whether or not that was the case we still don't know. What we do know is that this baby named Jones became the plantation blacksmith and would one day own the land to which he was marketed and that it would be the dwelling place of his issue to this day.

Before moving on to the Clark residence we stopped at the site of the blacksmith shop. An anachronism. The heavy old anvil was still in its place, dented and scarred from the pounding it took from Robert Clark's great-granddaddy's hammer so many years ago. The furnace is gone but the vise is still there alongside the anvil. I imagined hearing my own grandfather hammering plow points, smelled the smoke from the bellows I had pumped to heat the metal to workability.

We rode along in silence for a while. Robert Clark was telling me more of his history than I could appropriate at once.

When we began talking again, we envisioned what the slave great-great-grandmother of Representative Robert George Clark might have been like. In our supposing she became somehow reminiscent of the Song of Solomon. She was, we supposed, young, dainty, seductive in her innocence, comely in her resplendent blackness. We imagined the plantation wife to have been past middle years, also attractive in her time, a time gone by. Highbred but churlish, perhaps pietistic in her ebbing passion, humiliated by the forfeiture of her nuptial bed to a slave woman. Of the planter class husband, the white great-great-grandsire of the Mississippi speaker pro tem, we ventured nothing good at all. Except that in some kind of convoluted sensibility he spared his son the life of a field hand. Had he not done that, his and Rachel's son would not have had the wherewithal when the war ended to purchase the Jones plantation. He had saved the dollar per acre he paid for the land from odd jobs as a blacksmith during the war years when white blacksmiths of the yeomanry were away. No matter, from this act of unlicensed love, there came a line of consequential humanity.

Robert George Clark was not the first black registrant in Holmes County in 1967. He was a schoolteacher who would have been summarily fired if he had tried. Ironically, his father had been the last black citizen to have his name stricken from the registration roles years earlier. Some thought Robert Clark was a new-fashioned Uncle Tom when he was not the first to appear at the head of a protest march. Few question his judgment now. He was not biding his time, waiting for a propitious moment that would serve his immediate purposes. He was a pragmatist in the fray for the long haul, knowing that the outcome would not rest on the drama of marches to the courthouse, as altogether necessary as the marches were.

Being with Robert Clark made me think about my own upbringing in Amite County. Just a hundred miles to the south. I was three years old when he was born. We were both children of the twenties. A time when nothing slept and justice was yet deferred. I had only glimpses of the locked doors. Only occasional casual signals from my grandfather that all was not right. Robert Clark had heard of the locked doors from the day he was born. He knew well where the locks were and the nature of the keys.

"What were you thinking about as you strolled through the corridor of your neighbors and into your first voting booth?" I asked as we turned off Highway 17 and headed toward Clark Road in the Ebenezer community.

He laughed. "Uh, huh. Uh, huh. A lot of things. I reckon the first thing I was wondering was what it looked like on the inside of that voting booth. Looked like an executioner's booth at the time." He laughed again and fell silent.

"What else?" I said after a pause.

"Yeah. Well, I thought about Paw, my granddaddy. All the things he taught me. I thought about how he told me things would change but that we couldn't run away the way he had. When the man said he was going to kill him but wound up shooting over his head. Said there would be lots of shots fired over our heads . . . just people bluffing. But we had to stand. Even if they weren't shooting over our heads. Yeah, I was thinking about how I wished he was there walking toward that dark-looking stall with me."

"He would have enjoyed voting, wouldn't he?" I asked.

"Well, you know. I was just thinking about that. He had voted plenty of times. Plenty of times." I didn't understand. "Voting was what got him in trouble in the first place. We could vote after slavery, you know. Only when we were taking the thing over did the shooting begin and Paw had to run."

"Are you afraid that will happen again?" I asked.

"Paw didn't run because he was afraid," he answered. "He ran to save the life of a friend. I didn't run for office just for my own sake. Not alone anyhow. For us all. If I'm not free, you're not free." I knew what he meant.

Before we reached Clark Road and Speaker Clark's residence, he had stopped so we could walk the site of his first school. The land had once belonged to a black family but no longer. A massive red oak spread its boughs over the area. He described how the students had sat under that same tree to eat their sack lunches. The one-room building had long since fallen down. We walked a ways down the dirt gravel road that brought him to school each day, then back to where the little schoolhouse had stood. Poignant grunts punctuated his words as he described in detail what the schooling had been like. The shade of the huge tree seemed to prompt his memory. "This old tree has lots of childhood memories," he said. But it wasn't telling them. At least not to the white visitor. It presides over its secrets with dignity and assurance.

Eventually we reached his house on Clark Road. He had stopped the motor and several of his hunting dogs were yelping and leaping on the side of the door.

"Saying hello?" I asked.

"Something like that," he said.

He continued a sort of monologue about what he was thinking about that day he voted for the first time, stopping and starting as the random thoughts flickered and left. "I thought about the night Paw died. I was in boarding school in Durant. He was ninety-nine years, four months, and seventeen days old. I was sixteen. Wish he could have lived to see me now but he would be Methuselah by now." He remembered the funeral as the biggest he had ever seen at Pleasant Green. "Lots of crying. Lots of crying."

There was another pause. "I know you think that's a lot to think about on such a short walk from the door to the booth. But you know how stuff just runs through your mind." I said I did.

"He's buried over at the McBee Cemetery. We'll ride over there directly." There was another pause, the dogs still yelping. Mrs. Clark was smiling and waving from the porch.

"And I thought about the time my mamma died." He had already told me about his mother's death but he repeated much of it. Almost as if it happened the day before. Again he was in school in Durant. There was no high school for Negroes on their side of the county and after the eighth grade students either arranged to go to Durant or Lexington or dropped out. Most dropped out. Not the Clark family. Robert had an aunt who lived in Durant. He boarded with her and came home on weekends.

His mother was frail and his father was teaching school in Lynchfield, a plantation school on the Delta side of Holmes County. Robert would ride the train or bus the twenty miles from Durant to Pickens and then walk the eight more miles to his home in the Ebenezer community.

Robert well remembers that particular weekend. A sizeable herd of their hogs were out and it was his job to find them and get them back before returning to school. He found them in Yazoo County, two hours away. On Monday morning, when it was time to leave to go to school, his mother called him to her bedside. "It wasn't a maudlin thing," he said. Just a lengthy mother-to-son visit. He remembers, however, thinking it was a leave-taking unlike the others. Next day Robert was in government class, taught by the principal. That classroom was next to the office. When the phone rang, Robert Clark knew it was for him. He didn't have to pick up the receiver on the wall phone to know what the caller would say. "Mother is dead. Best you come on home." He caught the next bus to Pickens and then walked on home.

We continued to sit in front of his house. Silent for what seemed a long time. Representative Clark reliving. Silently now. Finally, "But I never been a crybaby," he said, opening the door and moving to embrace his wife. His words were strangely unconvincing.

The house is not more than twenty feet from the road. Clark Road. There are only two other houses on the road. The road ends a few hundred yards from Representative Clark's house. A large American flag flies from a front porch staff.

"This is the room I was born in," he said as Mrs. Clark led us into a neatly kept, well-furnished kitchen. "Of course, it was a bedroom then."

Robert George Clark, speaker pro tem of the Mississippi House of Representatives, was born in this humble place on October 3, 1928. It was a political year. In a real sense it was a turning point in American politics. For the first time a Roman Catholic was running for president. Democrat Alfred E. Smith, governor of New York and a Catholic, was pitted against Herbert Clark Hoover, a Quaker Republican. Hoover had risen to prominence the year before Clark was born when he headed the relief efforts for victims of the catastrophic Mississippi River flood of 1927. That flood had forced close to a million people from their homes. The death toll was in the thousands. The Red Cross fed approximately seven hundred thousand people for months. The house in which Clark was born was above the flood level but he remembers the stories, especially those of how Negro citizens were literally once more in a state of peonage. Police would arrest them wherever they were found, and if they refused to work the levees, they were jailed until they agreed. Because Hoover headed the relief work, his name was headlined throughout the nation daily. Despite the publicity few believe he would have beat Al Smith without the religious prejudice. Mr. Clark compared the prejudice against Catholics to that against people of color. He spoke of the irony of so many blacks who opposed John F. Kennedy thirty-two years later for the same reason.

As Mrs. Clark finished preparing iced tea and a snack on individual trays, he showed me the remainder of the house. There is the archetypal hallway that divides the house. There is a parlor across from the kitchen where we would soon sit and visit.

"This is where my mamma sat and sewed my clothes by the light of a coal oil lamp."

The last room on the left is Representative Clark's office. It is cluttered even more than my own. "Most of my stuff is at the capitol," he said. "This was the kitchen before we remodeled."

"And you've lived here all your life?" I asked.

"All my life. Except when I was away in school. My parents built this house after they were married. Moved from the old house on the back of the property. We'll go there in a while."

IV

Robert Clark was a runt until he was fifteen years old. His health was good. He was energetic, bright, ambitious without pretension, mischievous. Because of his closeness to Grandpa Clark he might have been seen as the family pet. Someone once said "Gracious!" when they saw him for the first time and that became his nickname throughout his childhood. It was not until he was in college that he was called Clark. Robert George was not the only grandchild William Clark, or "Paw," as he was called, had. Robert had one brother and one sister, children of his mother. His father remarried and another son was born. There were also cousins. The only way he was different from the others was that he wouldn't grow until his early teens. He laughs now, saying that after he started growing, his head and sometimes neck and chest would run into a wire fence or tree limb that he had been used to walking under without bending. Such was the rate of his growth.

Because he was small he didn't have to go to the fields to work with the other children and both parents. That meant he was at home alone with Granddaddy William Clark. Robert

George Clark would go on to three universities and have many educational experiences. But at no place and under no schoolmaster would he have a better teacher than William Clark, a slave who survived slavery but as a freedman narrowly missed assassination. William Clark was a deeply spiritual man, grandfatherly patient, wise. He and his grandson knew a friendship as well as a kinship. On summer days they lolled in the shade at the end of cotton rows. One too old, the other too young and too little to work the fields. On clear autumn days they walked the dense woods of what had been the family homeplace since the Civil War ended and Henry Jones the slave became Henry Jones the plantation owner when he purchased it with the money he had made as a blacksmith during the war. On cold winter nights Robert Clark and his granddaddy, William Clark, lay sinking in thick feather mattresses under piles of handcrafted quilts. It was in those places and on those occasions that young Robert George heard the stories. In the stories William Clark ran again through the Big Black River swamp, young Robert Clark by his side. Robert the lad with William the old man listened in the night to the howls of coyotes, the euphonious music of katydids and whippoorwills, and watched the drift of the moon across the sky, leaving distorted shadows, winged nocturnal mammals diving for seemingly nonexistent prey; in the day they heard the bickering of troubled hawks and crows, and tree frogs affirming rain. With him he ate sheepshawls, beech mast, the translucent seeds of maypops, crab apples and papaws. In Gideon fashion Robert drank with Paw from clear crystal springs bubbling and rushing to replenish the Big Black. He learned of prayer and friendship as the grandfather did not take the nearest route from Clinton to Vicksburg but ran north a ways to the bend in the Big Black River where William and Jesse, as friends and for those hours equals, had shared a fishing hole, sharing then the same waters with their naked bodies, swimming, bathing; equals still. Robert the child, in his fantasy, knelt with his grandfather a long time beside the river and prayed for the soul and safety of Jesse, the friend who had spared his life. Lad followed man as they climbed tall trees and watched in the gloaming for strangers who might foil the escape. On their bellies they crawled from crosstie to crosstie on the railroad bridge spanning the river rather than risk casting a silhouette in the moonlight. The lad heard the grandfather pray by name for all his neighbors and fellow workers in the Republican Party in their quest for political equality. Lastly, a prayer for personal forgiveness for leaving his people. The grandson still remembers the ache in the old man's heart when he talked of deserting his people for his own safety. It was a guilt which plagued him all his life and it was on such occasions that he would say there would be change, deliverance, at the hands of his grandson and the other young. He would not have been surprised that his grandson would one day be Speaker Pro Tempore Robert George Clark of the Mississippi House of Representatives.

Representative Clark talks with gratitude of how his Grandfather Clark organized the Baptist Church in the Ebenezer community and named it Pleasant Green, the same name he had given the church in Clinton, the one he felt he had left behind. The old man explained his pleasure at seeing the church rolls without the offensive lettering FMC (free man of color) or FWC following each name. It was at Pleasant Green in Ebenezer where Robert Clark was converted at the age of five and baptized in a nearby pond. Black folks' church and black folks' land and pond. It was at Pleasant Green that Robert Clark first learned of civil rights, of equality and the ballot. He remembers with awe and amusement the way Pleasant Green would be filled with people at revival meetings or weeknight services until Reverend Clark started talking about racial injustices. Then the congregation, many fearful that their landlords might have spies present, began leaving until there would be almost no one left. Robert Clark learned as a lad that life would be rough, unfair for him, but he also learned that he was as good as anyone.

William Clark worked on the river for three years after leaving Clinton, settling in Greenville. In 1878 a death-dealing yellow fever epidemic swept through the Delta and adjoining counties. Clark, still with no ties to hinder his leaving, walked through the Delta, up the loess bluffs, and made his way to the flatland of Holmes County. Resourceful as always he signed on as a wage hand with Henry Jones, the blacksmith who had bought the plantation on which he had been a slave. Henry Jones would become the father-in-law of William Clark, although not without a vigorous demurrer. The objection was that William Clark was too dark. Clark's Creek Indian father, the father he never saw, and his African mother had bequeathed him a near-black skin. Henry Jones's father was the white planter in Alabama, so his complexion was light. Despite the objection the marriage did take place.

Robert George Clark is a paradigm for all my characters and for all of humankind. By extraction he is African. He is also Caucasian, for his great-grandaddy Jones was the son of a white planter. He is Asian if we accept the supposal that American Indians got to these shores via the Bering Strait. In a sense, racially he is the whole story. And sociologically people of color have always been the fundamental story of America. The American dilemma.

William had spoken of Moses to Jesse Furver when Furver was threatening to kill him. Later, in a perhaps innocent sequence of events, his grandson, Robert, seemed to be a faint but noticeable echo of some of the drama of Moses. As I listened to Robert, representative to the Mississippi legislature, I thought of it. Robert talked of seeing a strange and unexplainable light just as Moses did. Mr. Clark does not mention the comparison and only chuckled when I brought it up. He would never compare himself, even in jest, to a biblical character. He does, however, find the appearing of the light on two occasions mystifying. The lights were not like the burning bush of Moses but were unexplainable in the same fashion. Clark makes no effort to explain the lights. Simply describes the event. "I don't believe in haints," he says. "Not even signs and omens. I know only that on two occasions, each time on a clear and calm night, I saw a light nearby that couldn't be explained." And on each occasion his grandfather was nearby. "I saw the light again ten years later. This time the light was northwest of the house, approximately half a mile, not moving, almost to the top of the trees, and a large portion of the woods were lighted."

One such as I likes to believe that perhaps, just maybe, the unexplained lights were a signal that the one to whom they appeared would one day be a leader of his people.

There was also a snake that lay on the ground between the house and mailbox. It often taunted the young boy, his grandfather always nearby to send the snake scurrying for the deep weeds. Robert Clark never alluded to the snake Moses saw. Nor did I. But who's to say? Stranger things have happened.

There was never a question about education among the Clarks and Joneses. They would get all they could and learn in any fashion they could. When William Clark left the Delta and got a job working for Henry Jones for five dollars a month he found a family as literate as he. Only the most heartless would now dispute that slavery was a cruel, evil, and unconscionable system that should never have been. Yet within the demonic formula there were those who felt an itch of decency. Some allowed, even encouraged, literacy.

Those to whom Henry Jones was sold were apparently among them, for he could read, write, and cipher when William Clark hired on. It is also possible that Henry Jones's white father, whose legal wife killed the planter's black lover, made as a condition of the sale not only that his son would not be a field slave but also that he would be educated. That, of course, is conjecture. Whatever the case William Clark went to work for a literate family, later married into it, and brought as his dowry a good mind and willing hands.

As we walked the old homeplace now, Robert Clark talked of when the old homeplace was new. What he says is of oral tradition, for it goes back a century and a half. I was most interested, at the time, in the circumstances and events of his running for office, being elected so soon after registering to vote. There were other things he had to tell me first. About how education, religion, and farming were the primary concerns of the Jones and Clark families. The two families become one. He talked about how his father home-schooled himself, got a high school equivalency diploma and attended Jackson State University, a forty-mile commute each day, and became a schoolteacher. He digressed to tell me about his closeness to his father and of the night his father died. It was as if he wanted me to know his father well. Robert was living at home then, in 1962. But there was something else I had to hear. Another digression. We were just walking and rambling, getting closer and closer to the family cemetery, the McBee Cemetery.

He told me again of how he happened to be the one who stayed on the family farm to take care of the elders and the business. He was just beginning his time at Jackson State following high school.

"My auntie and my daddy had asked me to come home for a family conference. I was worried as to what they wanted, afraid they had heard some rumor about some alleged indiscretion. Something I knew wasn't true. Anyway, what they wanted to talk about was my moving back home and operating all the family business. Home. Farm. Everything.

"'No. No. Not me. Please,' I argued. 'Not me. I don't like farm life. No good at it.'" In the end they convinced him to move back and operate the family business.

When the time came to move back permanently, he wanted to move his aging father out of the woods and onto a public road. When the weather was bad, he had to take the car two miles to the passable road and then walk home. His father would simply talk of family history. Joneses. Clarks.

Walking along he talked of the night his father died. He had moved back and was teaching and coaching in Lexington.

On this night he told his father he was going to Lexington to take some moving pictures of a friend's baby, and then to Porter's Place, a cafe and service station in town. His father said they were out of matches. "Don't forget the matches, son." When he got to the top of the hill coming back, almost home, he remembered he had forgotten the matches.

His father seemed all right when he gave him the matches. Big kitchen matches. Diamond brand matches.

"Thank you, son. See you in the morning."

"I got up during the night to go to the bathroom. Stumbled. Realized my father was lying on the floor. I called my brother in Memphis. My sister in Chicago."

We were standing on the edge of the little McBee graveyard now. "Daddy was in a coma. Before they got home he was dead." There was the kind of pause in the family account I had become accustomed to. Then, "And here he lies." Mrs. Clark stepped to her husband's side, took his hand and kissed it. The closeness between son and father had not gone away. The grief lingered, and Jo Ann Clark intuited her husband's need for comforting.

We moved among the graves. There were no mausoleums, no above-ground vaults, just stones memorializing a humble but proud people. The graves were not crowded, as in big city cemeteries. Somehow one does not think of this as a cemetery at all. This is a graveyard; a country graveyard, modest and soundless, awaiting that special morning. The scudding clouds cast vague shadows. The wind picked up and Mrs. Clark had to turn the wide-brimmed, fashionable straw hat into the wind. Like a sail.

Robert George Clark, speaker pro tempore of the Mississippi House of Representatives, identified each grave, even those with no markers. He said a few sentences about each one. I, of course, wanted to see the grave of Grandfather William Clark, the heroic ex-slave who never forgave himself for leaving his people in Hinds County but without whom this plot of ground in Holmes County would be lying fallow of his issue.

"This is his grave right here. Grandpa William. Paw. My, my. He taught me a lot." We moved a few steps forward. "Grandmother Clark is right here. Great-grandfather, Henry Jones. Great-grandmother, Rachel Jones. Great-uncle, Professor Henry Jones. Oh, I have to tell you about him sometime. Another great-uncle. Another Henry Jones. Great-aunt, Lucy Mitchell. A nephew, Thomas. He's right there."

Robert Clark sensed that I was having trouble making notes on all the graves as he identified them. Mrs. Clark led him a few feet and straightened a small vase on another grave. She patted her husband sympathetically and reassuringly, said something to him, then nudged him back near where I was standing.

"Get all that? Uh, huh? Uh, huh? Here's Aunt Rachel,

Uncle George, Uncle William. Uncle Eddie. Uncle Henry." He moved again. "And Grandfather William Henry Jones. Grandmother Sally." Three more aunts. "Aunt Amanda, Aunt Annie." Then off to one side. "And Aunt Mae Sula."

I had never heard the name Sula before. "Did you say Sula?" I asked.

"Well, yes. Mae Sula. Two words." He spelled them out. "Capital M-a-e. Then capital S-u-l-a. Mae Sula."

"He's still a schoolteacher," I remember thinking.

I asked if he knew the derivation of Sula. He said he had wondered the same thing years ago. He found out it was the feminine form of *sulaiman*. Arabic. North Africa. The word meant "peaceful." Thinking for a moment about Alex Haley and *Roots* I asked if he knew how far back the name Sula went in his family. He didn't.

Still curious about the name I checked further when I returned home. It was also from the Cherokee word *tsula*, meaning fox. Interesting, I thought. That she should have a Cherokee name in Choctaw country. But wait. *Tchula* was the Choctaw word for red fox. And Tchula was a town not far from Ebenezer, the birthplace of Aunt Sula and all the generations of Clarks and Joneses since slavery. I had never had much interest in etymology. Suddenly I did. Mae Sula. From North African Arabic to the Choctaw language to Mississippi English. Aunt Mae Sula. Pretty name.

Seeming to sense my next question he added, "Mother is buried in the New Canaan Cemetery beside her father. She requested it."

"Will you be buried here?" I asked.

"I'll be buried here. Right over there." He pointed to the grave of his first wife, Essie.

I was impressed with the genealogy and his ability to recite it. "Any of these families ever break up?" I asked. "Any divorces?"

He laughed heartily. "No, I guess we were too poor to break up. We needed one another too much." I thought for a moment of all I had read in recent years about disfunctional black families. Partly fact, mostly fiction, I mused.

"Here's one more," he added. There was a tiny grave but no marker. He said there would be one. There had been a still-born child. His mother named him Frederick Douglass. There I stood with Robert George Clark, the first black American to be elected to the Mississippi House of Representatives since Reconstruction. A relatively young, robust man filled with life and love of it. Standing beside the grave of Frederick Douglass, dead in the womb nearly three-quarters of a century ago. I thought of another Frederick Douglass who lived to maturity. Surely one of America's most energetic and effective abolitionists. Although his major vocation was for equal rights for his people, he stood with Susan B. Anthony, Elizabeth Cady Stanton, and others in the cause of women's rights as well. He shook the foundation of the nation and began the long back-pack toward freedom. Frederick Douglass. Brazen, brilliant, loquacious, long-suffering.

I asked Clark if his parents were aware of the significance of the name. He smiled, did not answer. Just looked at me, as a wise elder might respond to the simple question of a child.

Trying to cover my silly inquiry I quickly added, "I mean, it just seems the name Frederick Douglass would have been more appropriate for you."

Still there was no response. Perhaps he was thinking, "I'm quite content with the name I bear."

And rightly so. Robert Clark is not the animated, restless revolutionary that the nineteenth-century prophet was, yet he wrestles with the same principalities and powers, and with equal yearning for unconditional manumission. An estate that even now lies somewhere in the future, for, he had told me, "They accept us as politically equal now, economically equal, yet they don't quite accept us." I wondered if I, as a white man, even his close friend now, really understood.

Before we moved along I pondered the possible subliminal, perhaps extrasensory, influence of baby Frederick Douglass on Robert George the man. I recalled the strange lights, the mystical quality I had sensed in him when first we met. I marveled that a man could speak with such exactness of a grandfather who shaped him to the thing he is but not be haunted by a baby brother whose name fit the deeds of the elder brother. As we moved out of the cemetery, I couldn't shake the thought of one buried there named Frederick Douglass. Perhaps it was because my introduction to the elder Frederick Douglass had so shaped my adult life. I thought of how if there had not been that introduction to the Frederick Douglass of the nineteenth century, I would not then be standing near the grave of his namesake. My thoughts crossed the years to a troop ship bound for war in the South Pacific in 1943. I was an eighteen-year-old army private. A New Hampshire chaplain encouraged use of the ship's meager library to breach the boredom on the five-week voyage. In the life of an eighteen-year-old, five weeks spent rocking with the waves on the waters of the Pacific Ocean was a long time. Of the several books I read before we dropped anchor off New Caledonia Island, two made an impression on me that never went away. One was a short novel by Howard Fast, *Freedom Road*, a book my brother had sent me from Panama earlier and which I had saved in my barracks bag for the trip. The other one, recommended to me by the chaplain, maybe because of my unmistakable southern, country-boy accent, was *My Bondage and My Freedom* by Frederick Douglass. I had never heard of the man. His name had never been mentioned in the small rural school I had attended in south Mississippi. I was overwhelmed by what I read. It was, for me, epiphanal, a deliverance, and from that moment on I knew my life would never be the same. Even as a callow youth from the yeomanry of the most remote area of

Mississippi I knew that Frederick Douglass the abolitionist was speaking to my own captivity. Near the grave of a tiny baby named for him I felt that he was near. I assumed that it was William Clark, grandfather of my host, who had named him. William Clark was a contemporary and doubtless the young William had heard the stories. Too bad his cause of unalloyed equality and freedom for his people had not prevailed. If it had I would not be standing here, far from home, researching a book about Robert Clark, who did not have the disposition of Douglass but who shared the yearning of the original.

In most ways William and Frederick were more alike than Robert and Frederick. As children both William and Frederick had stooped to eat cornmeal mush from a trough like hogs. William did not go on to walk with the famed and mighty of the earth as Frederick did but the parallels were plentiful. Both men were deeply religious. Both had a mild flirtation with the institutional church, both men learned the nature of institutions: that they were all, religious or not, self-loving, self-preserving, and concerned foremost with self-survival, and though the two men's basic allegiance to the faith remained, they moved in other channels for the bulk of their accomplishments. At least Frederick Douglass did.

I let it pass.

Finally, not as an afterthought but more like a treasure he had reserved, Robert Clark added, "And here's my first wife,

Essie, mother of our sons, Robert and Bryant." I glanced at his wife, Jo Ann. Her countenance was one of approbation and pride. I was not surprised. Back at the residence she had made Essie and the sons the first for me to see among the pictures on the walls.

Robert Clark had been seasoned by his grandfather to do something to improve the lot of his people but the thought of doing it through elected offices was slow in coming. Until the patience of African Americans had been exhausted and people turned more and more to the streets in a mass movement of protest, he had thought primarily in terms of education, ministry in the church, or the business world. He knew that he was well equipped to run for public office, but what chance was there to be elected in a county in which not one black citizen was registered to vote? He had been seasoned by hard work as a child and the experiences of the Great Depression. And by being black in a draconian culture where race dictated every area of behavior. Growing up poor and white during those years of economic depression was hard. Growing up black was worse because the opportunities for escaping the deprivation were fewer. Yet as Mr. Clark and I compared notes one day we found many similarities that had not to do with color. His family, like mine, made two or three trips a year to town. His to Lexington, twelve miles away, mine to McComb, the same distance. We remembered getting up before daybreak Christmas morning and finding a few apples and oranges, a small toy, shooting a few firecrackers. And in both households there was the seemingly inevitable hoop cheese our fathers bought each Christmas.

Movies were not allowed by either family because interpretation of Scripture was that to go to the picture show was serving idols. Both my parents and his allowed ball playing and swimming, except on Sundays, but no dancing, no card playing ever. Neither family had a radio until we were twelve or fourteen years old. Not because a radio was considered sinful, like movies, but because we couldn't afford one.

The most telling radio memory for both of us was the night of a Joe Lewis–Max Schmeling prizefight. Robert Clark's family walked three miles to a white family's house where the radio was placed in the window. While the white folks listened inside the house, the black folks sat or stood in the yard. My family went to a cousin's house where only whites had gathered.

Mr. Clark remembers the jubilation of the black folks when Joe Lewis knocked out Schmeling. Whistles, cheering, backslapping, laughter. He remembers as vividly the stony silence among the white folks inside. Troubling, but it did not stop the celebration outside the window.

I remember only the prolonged silence when Max Schmeling went down. Finally an uncle saying, "I know he's a kraut

but it just ain't right for a darkie to knock out a white man."
Then my brother's whimsical rejoinder. "Well, one just did."
He was censured. "Watch your mouth, young man."

Our people—Joe Lewis's people and my people—were four
years from war with Schmeling's people. But the thing called
race reared its head again, like an anaconda, coiled and prevailing, squeezing logic from the response to a prizefight.

There were also many dissimilarities between Representative Clark's childhood and mine. I never had a sheriff point a
pistol in my face and threaten to blow my brains out for saying
"uh, huh" to a white woman. I didn't have to stay up all night
with a shotgun in my lap because I had put a sack of groceries
in the wrong car and the woman said they would come that
night to settle it because she said I had sassed her. (His father
was teaching school away from home and his mother was
sick. All night the boy prayed they wouldn't come and they
didn't.) When I was a boy I didn't have to walk to school while
children of another race passed me on the road in a bus, throwing objects out the window.

Through it all the Clark children got a solid foundation for
further schooling. The father had studied correspondence
courses at home and gotten a high school equivalency
diploma. He also tutored his black neighbors in fundamental
subjects, and the Clark children often sat around the fire with
the adult students and listened. He attended Jackson State
University and became a teacher.

There was an elementary school near the Clark farm that had been established by the Rosenwald Fund, one among the six thousand one- and two-room schools that dotted the southern countrysides and played a major role in uplifting black children from a life of illiteracy. In 1912 Julius Rosenwald, a Russian immigrant and president of Sears, Roebuck and Co., wanted to do something to improve the lot of Negro children in what he saw as the disfigured soul of the South.

> He that putteth not out his money to usury, nor taketh reward against the innocent. He that doeth these things shall never be moved. —Psalm 15:5

Influenced, it was said, by those words of the Fifteenth Psalm and in consultation with his friends Booker T. Washington and, later, Robert R. Moton, Washington's successor as principal of Tuskegee Institute, Rosenwald devised a plan to establish schools in rural areas of the South. With Rosenwald's resources a fund was established, administered by Tuskegee Institute, to construct one- and two-room schoolhouses and employ a teacher, sometimes two, for each school. The contribution to the advancement of Negro education was inestimable.

Robert Clark attended one of the schools but had already been to public school for two years. That was a one-room school, set in a grove of cutover scrubby pines and dappled oaks, where his aunt Annie Clark taught. At first the young Robert didn't want to go to school. Being in the same room with fifteen- and sixteen-year-old boys when he was small, even for a six-year-old, upset him. His mother would walk him to school and when she turned around he turned to follow her. Sometimes the doting Grandfather Clark would leave the house to walk the lad to school but they would hang out in the woods all day. He teaching. The boy learning. Or perhaps boy and old man teaching; boy and old man learning. In any event it was an important part of young Robert's unfolding.

The aunt was a strict disciplinarian and so was Mrs. Clark. When he balked at memorizing the multiplication tables, she punished him and made him learn the tables from two through twelve in one night's session. When he became adjusted to the routine, he was an excellent student and liked school.

Jackson State was difficult for him at first. An operation that resulted in the loss of sight in one eye had put him behind in the last two years of high school. He had to study hard at first to compensate. In addition to his studies he worked on campus for half of his room and board and another job for twenty-five cents an hour. Because his favorite subject had been English and because he was bright, he was able to close the gap. In high school, and from his father, he had learned how to take notes and conduct research, proper study habits in general. He borrowed books from other students because he could afford few of his own. He ran track but not at first, on scholarship. He excelled in the sport and laughs today, saying that because of the blindness in his left eye he could better hear other runners gaining on him. He credits track with teaching him the art of competition.

Ironically, Clark's first intense experience with rigid segregation was in Jackson, not rural Holmes County. Because his family owned the land they worked and did not depend on whites for their livelihood, they did not have to come into close daily contact with whites. Even socially, as children, relationships were more relaxed. In Jackson segregation was rigid in every aspect. There were certain areas of Jackson where blacks simply did not go. A friend of Clark's was walking down a white folks' section of Capitol Street and a policeman picked him up. Jackson State's president, Jacob Reddix, when called by the student, went to the jail. When he asked with what his student was charged, the officer said, "Well, we caught him in the white folks' area." There was a pause, perhaps the officer wondering how he would explain "white folks' area" in legal terms. He continued, "And we charged him with reckless eyeballing." He probably meant that the young man had cast an eye in the direction of a white woman, a grievous offense in the Mississippi of the forties. President Reddix knew how to finesse white folks by pretending to be on their side. After sneaking a wink at the student, with a straight face he exploded, "Now, young man, you know that at

Jackson State we don't teach, and we don't tolerate, reckless eyeballing." Hearing Representative Clark's hearty laugh at the telling of the tale that happened a long time ago leads one to suspect it was an art form he, too, found useful before he rose to prominence in what had once been the world of white folks' politics.

Although he would later return and graduate, Robert Clark, because of a special curriculum arrangement, left Jackson State and began teaching school at Louise. (There was never any question about his returning to finish.) Louise was a Delta village of about four hundred people, located north of Yazoo City in Humphreys County. The only jobs were cotton plantation jobs. Even most elementary schools for Negroes were plantation schools. Because teaching school was the best employment well-educated Negroes could get, black children at the elementary level generally got better schooling than whites. A black person with a master's degree could be an elementary school teacher. A white with the same degree had options paying far more.

Although teaching and coaching in an understaffed rural school was a full-time job, there was time for reflection. He began thinking seriously about becoming a missionary to Africa. He had heard returning missionaries talk of the needs and what life was like there. He felt led to go to Nairobi. His church's mission board accepted him, but school was in session, and, characteristically conscientious, he would not leave his students. Instead he decided to go to graduate school the following year.

He wanted to prove that he could compete in a white world, but Mississippi had no graduate programs Negroes were allowed to attend. Instead there was a regional program which would pay for students to attend graduate and professional schools in northern states. Called the Southern Regional Education Board, it was primarily a device to avoid lawsuits from Negro citizens on the grounds that they did not have access to graduate programs, a violation of the equal protection clause to the U.S. Constitution. It worked for many years, and numerous black students became attorneys, medical doctors, and educators in universities superior to those which would not accept them in the southern states.

Clark was admitted to Notre Dame, UCLA, and Michigan State. He chose Michigan State because the curriculum was more attuned to the field of education. In addition Michigan State had a history of outstanding black athletes. Because Jackson State was not accredited at the time, Clark's admission was probationary. He excelled as a student and when the probation period was over, he was accepted as a regular student.

At Michigan State the young teacher learned that the transgressions of the white world extended far beyond the borders of his native Mississippi. Although he had every intention of returning to Mississippi to continue teaching, he saw that

Michigan was really Mississippi without signs. White students could live in East Lansing. Blacks only in Lansing, unless they lived on campus. When white coeds let it be known that they would welcome dating the handsome dark-skinned man, white boys let it be equally known that they would not look with favor on it. Generally he was the only black man in each class so social life was a lonely trail.

When he was offered an assistantship to remain at the university for a doctorate, he turned it down. When a school system in Michigan's Upper Peninsula was experimenting with integrating their staff positions, the Mississippian was offered a teaching post at four times the salary in Humphreys County. The school board in the Upper Peninsula had the idea that a Negro teacher from the South would make things go more smoothly. They told him it was much like Mississippi. Again Robert Clark turned it down. Might as well go back to his own students. He had had enough of white students who saw him as a black man from benighted Mississippi while copying off his test paper.

Some years later he would have similar experiences while at Harvard with a teaching fellowship at the John F. Kennedy School of Government. By then he had become a prominent member of the Mississippi House of Representatives. He lectured on southern politics from Reconstruction through the civil rights movement. Students were more interested in race and prejudice as it existed in the South than in what he wanted to teach them. "If you wanted to be a black racist, you could get a large following in a hurry," he says today. He soon tired of it and found himself defensive about his native state. He agreed that Mississippi was behind economically and educationally but found that one had a greater chance of being harmed in Boston than in Jackson, Mississippi. He would recount anecdotes like the one about reckless eyeballing when he was a student at Jackson State but follow that by telling them that today a black person could walk all over Jackson but there were places in Boston where blacks couldn't go. "Try going to Southie if you're my color," he told them. He did not deny the racism in Mississippi, for he had known it firsthand. "But let's talk about Boston," he would say. "You don't live in Mississippi."

At the time there was an outstanding black athlete in Boston. In the first half of a football game his performance had been great and his team was winning. At halftime he was shot and permanently paralyzed.

"Do such things happen in your state?" he was asked.

"Of course. But we're not in my state."

As a teaching fellow he had the same privileges as students and faculty. He registered for several courses and found them boring.

"Didn't they see you as overly defensive and protecting about Mississippi?" I asked him.

"Certainly. But I was there to teach. I had been all over the world and could refute their scorn of Mississippi." Unusual pedagogy, perhaps, for a man who had been a victim of the racism his Harvard compatriots wanted to hear him relate.

But as he said, he was there to teach.

Clark was not disillusioned by the racism in Lansing and Cambridge. He had suspected all along that bigotry was not confined to his native Mississippi. His experience was important in one way, however. It was while he was at Harvard that he abandoned the idea of becoming a missionary to Africa. There was more than enough "converting" to do in his own country.

Long before the Harvard experience Robert Clark learned that integrity in teaching had its hazards. A high school in which he was principal got a small library for the first time. One of the books had a black rabbit and a white rabbit hopping together. His building superintendent brought a message from the county superintendent of education that the principal should pull that book from the library. It might give the children the idea that black children were supposed to play with white children. Tiring of the procrustean bed in which he had been forced to lie as a competent educator, Clark responded, "Tell the superintendent that if he wants the damn book pulled, he can come pull it himself." He was not, of course, rehired the following year.

From there he went to Thomastown in Leake County. He was coach and principal there for two years. It was there that he decided to honor the commitment he had made upon graduating from high school to be head of the household.

During the five years he was teacher and coach at Lexington Attendance Center, an all-black school, Holmes County was experiencing the civil rights movement at its crest. As a teacher in the public school system, an employee of the county, Mr. Clark was more of a supporter of the civil rights activities than he was an active participant. When the county sheriff routinely picked up young people wearing Martin Luther King buttons, took them to the courthouse and took the buttons away from them, the word got around that they could wear them in Coach Clark's classes. The students would pin them underneath a collar or lapel and as soon as they got to his class the buttons were uncovered. It troubled him that he didn't feel free to march with the marchers. But he was a pragmatist. He knew that for the long haul it was going to take many people playing many different roles to reach the goal of freedom. One misstep and he would be out. It was not a matter of biding his time. He knew that at some point he would make a political move. But he had to have a base.

Even without being a marcher or leader in the movement, he got in trouble. The ludicrous black rabbit and white rabbit episode was not the only time. While at Lexington Attendance Center he went before the board of education and asked for the establishment of adult education classes. Members of the board saw that as a subterfuge for teaching voter education. They told him that if the superintendent of education wanted an adult education program in the system, it would be done. Clark responded that the next time he came before them he would be superintendent of education. He did consider running for that office. Representative J. P. Love, the man Clark would eventually defeat for a seat in the state legislature, worked to get a bill passed that would change the system from one with an elected superintendent of education to one in which the person was appointed by the county board of education. That would mean no Negro would be appointed to the office. The county board was all white. The man would regret his success in that effort. If Clark could not run for superintendent of education, an office for which he was eminently qualified, then he would seek another. After toying with the idea of campaigning for sheriff and finding that another black citizen had the inside track on that office, he decided, well . . . why not? Why not run for the office held by the man responsible for making it impossible for him to be superintendent of education? Robert George Clark was and is a gentleman. He is not a vindictive person. But he did see the irony in that scenario.

Other fortuitous events seemed to work to nudge Clark in the direction of entering politics full time. With no contract at Lexington, Clark needed a job. And a base. The furniture store he owned in Lexington was not sufficient. Saints Junior College was a small two-year school operated by the Church of God in Christ. The mother church for that denomination was in Lexington. Clark was hired as director of adult education, a position that would serve him well in establishing a fertile political base.

V

By 1967 it was no longer possible to prevent black citizens from registering to vote. The system that had stood watch over the courthouse doors like the Praetorian Guard of the Roman emperors had fallen. Not since 1877, when President Rutherford B. Hayes pulled federal troops out of the South, had there been such rapid and radical political change. The Voting Rights Act passed under President Lyndon Johnson was being enforced, and daily the likelihood was increasing of a black majority on the registration rolls.

Coach Clark, as hundreds of young adults called him, had registered in 1966 without incident, and announced that he would be a candidate for representative from District Sixteen, the office held by the man who had made it impossible for him to seek the office of superintendent of education. Ironically, he would later be offered that appointment when the public schools had become all black. It would be a vehement segregationist in the legislature who would talk him out of accepting it, because he, by then, wanted him in the legislature. Clark declined because it would have meant resigning from the house of representatives, and he didn't want another black person to have to suffer as he had as the only black in the legislature.

Getting enough registered voters to sign the qualifying petition was not a problem. Having to defend the authenticity of each one was. Much of the challenging of signers was no more than harrassment, an effort to scare petitioners and potential signers. It was also time consuming for a candidate pressed for time and with few resources. Although he was a native of the county, most of his adult life had been spent elsewhere. That, however, did not mean he was not well known. He had been a teacher, coach, and referee, and then director of Project Second Start, the federally funded adult education program at Saints Junior College, and there were few people of color who did not know him by name or by sight.

One ploy used by his opposition to challenge petitioners was for a planter or landlord to say he knew that such and such person was illiterate because the person lived on his place and didn't know how to sign his or her name. Mr. Clark had a built-in rebuttal.

"I know that he can sign his name. Can read and write."

"How do you know?"

"Because I taught him how."

Many of the challenged ones had been Mr. Clark's students in Project Second Start.

Things like precise addresses, exact spelling, full middle name instead of initial—any technicality was used to reduce the number on the petition. None of it accomplished the goal.

Sometimes efforts backfired. It was reported that the incumbent had given two civil rights workers ("outsiders") money to see that Clark was defeated. The youthful activists liked the good life and found a way to use the money without hurting Clark. Robert George Clark was duly qualified and the campaigning began.

District Sixteen, Post One included all of Holmes County. Later, in an effort to defeat Clark for reelection, the lines would be redrawn. That, also, would not work to defeat him.

Holmes County was mostly villages, plantations, and small farms, from the flatland down the loess bluffs and well into the Delta. From the eastern county-line towns of West, Durant, Pickens, and Goodman, the Sixteenth District extended westward through Ebenezer, Lexington, and Tchula, then northward across the Chicopa Creek to Cruger. It began on a line with the Illinois Central Railroad that snaked, smoked, and whistled its way from New Orleans to Chicago. A few miles to the south was the place where Casey Jones, the legendary railroad engineer, lost his life. Other than that, the red clay and loess bluff regions of Mississippi had little drama to commend them.

A black man running for a state office would at least add theater to a prosaic era of the region's modern history. What would as recently as ten years earlier have been as unthinkable as nuclear weapons would have been in 1863 was actually happening. A black man was a candidate for an important state office with odds to win. People would turn out at rallies just to see a black man campaigning for office.

District Sixteen was a lot of acreage to cover. But Robert Clark knew the terrain. He was about to start a perilous journey. He was aware that black folks still got killed for "getting out of their place." He took precautions. He did not come home by the same route each time. There were many threats by phone and some nights he simply left the phone off the hook. He never walked before windows at night. Sometimes word would come to him not to show up at a certain meeting. Then he would have to decide if it was subterfuge to keep him away or someone with an authentic warning. A white man asked an elderly black man, "What would happen if Robert Clark ain't around at election time?" "If Robert Clark ain't around at election time, whole lot of white folks won't be around either. Not just poor whites either." Mr. Clark assumes now that if someone had death in mind for him such statements cooled the passions. It would be difficult. But he had no children, was still a bachelor, and both parents he had moved home to care for were dead. He would be about it.

Much of it would be fun.

He decided to run as an independent. To run as a Democrat would have required a lot of red tape plus running in a primary. He knew it would be difficult to get some people who had never voted once to understand that they must vote twice.

In addition, sharecroppers, tenant farmers, and wage hands might be subject to further intimidation between the primary and the general election.

He ran as assignee of the Freedom Democratic Party but did not depend on the FDP to carry his campaign. Robert Clark was a loner but he was also gregarious. Since almost everyone in the county knew him, he didn't have to cultivate new acquaintances. He worked in and through the Freedom Democratic Party but also around it. The fact that the Mississippi Freedom Democratic Party was the most powerful black political movement Mississippi had known since Reconstruction did not mean it was without disputants. The competition and disagreements between the NAACP and COFO continued even though the NAACP was a member of COFO. There was animosity between some professional blacks and the FDP. Also, some of the black middle class, those who had formerly had the prestige within the black community, felt that the FDP was made up of too many unlearned, unsophisticated, even illiterate people. Robert Clark knew this and was careful not to hang his campaign totally on the FDP.

Wherever people gathered, Robert Clark would find them. Greasy Spoon, Green Lantern, Chicken Shack, Pigs Place. And churches. He knew that ministers were vital to his success. In the recent past many of them had been considered irrelevant Uncle Toms. When Clark attended their gatherings, he was appreciated, was told that they had generally been ignored and that they appreciated his considering them as men of influence and that they would help him.

No place was too sacred or too profane for him. At nightclubs frequented by black neighbors on Saturday nights, he was discreet in his approach. He would check with the manager, who on every occasion would turn off the big Seeberg. Robert Clark never spoke more than forty-five seconds, saying something along the lines of: "Most of you know me but for those who don't my name is Robert Clark. I'm running for representative from this county. I thank you for listening to me and I won't take up much of your time. I would appreciate your support. If you're not registered to vote we'll help you do it. I know you're here to have a good time and I'm glad to see you enjoying yourselves. Hope to see you at the polls and hope you'll vote for me."

Generally that was all. The jukebox was started and the party continued as the candidate made his way through the crowd, greeting old friends, shaking hands with new ones.

Sometimes there would be unexpected endorsement and praise by an intoxicated patron, as in one club when the music from the jukebox was restarted, then immediately stopped. A husky woman wearing western boots and faded jeans with an extra-wide belt and heavy Bulldozer buckle bumbled to the front. Mr. Clark recognized her as a woman who had grown up in the Ebenezer community but had moved to the Delta to be the personal driver for a large plantation owner. He also remembered her as a woman who could hold her own in any encounter. Verbal or physical. She had unplugged the jukebox. With a slight slur she spoke to the hushed crowd. After addressing them with some well-chosen barnyard words she shouted, "Wait a minute. Now I know this boy. Knowed him as 'Gracious.' We growed up together back in the hills. I knowed him back at Ebenezer and I knowed his family. I want every damn one of you to vote for him and if you don't I'll be back and. . . ."

She concluded what might have been her first political address with a stern warning as to which part of their anatomy they should be prepared to defend if they didn't heed her advice.

The crowd broke into wild cheers and applause. Robert Clark knew the woman's admonition would be remembered on election day.

Next morning Robert Clark was visiting churches.

He tried to tailor his speeches to fit the audience. If speaking to teachers he talked about fair employment, salaries for Negro teachers equal to those of whites. When speaking to a church audience he talked of justice, relating the justice of today to that in the Bible. He never spelled out his entire platform. He counseled other black candidates who might be on the slate with him to do the same. His finish always was "You're very important to me and I need your help. I can't win this battle without you."

He learned to be good at flattery. He heard that an influential, powerful black lady had said, "Why should I vote for a trifling nigger? I get along all right with the white politicians."

Clark went directly to her. "You're very outstanding in this county. I'm coming to you for advice and guidance. I'm new at this. There are a whole lot of things that you know that I don't. I've got to have your advice and guidance if I'm to be successful."

Robert Clark says now, "It was all over." She went to bat for him. Organized a telephone pool in her social circle and kept in touch with the campaign.

He learned what people meant by a community and what was meant by neighborhood. A community was a circle of people with interests, professions, or something of essence in common. There was the granted, inclusive black community. Within that was the landholding community, the cliques of lodges, fraternities, and civic clubs, the church community, the community of laborers, sharecroppers, and wage hands, and many others. A neighborhood was a geographic entity. Where the people lived. He could safely address or contact one community or subcommunity without fear of offending another. But a neighborhood was a different matter. If he didn't have time to stop at one house, the word got out. So if he couldn't stop at all the houses in a neighborhood, he waited until another day when he had time for every family.

"Clark for Representative" rallies became social events. Even some white folks would come to satisfy their curiosity. And obviously some were convinced, because he received a middling number of white votes.

He was good at demographics. Knew where which people could be found. Some could be seen only at civil rights meetings. Some only at their church. Some at home, night spots and cafes. Others only on the streets. Television campaigning was impossible for him. And with no money for radio or newspaper appeals he took his campaign directly to the people, directing his message to individual communities and individuals within a neighborhood. It wasn't easy but it worked.

His was not a hate campaign. Despite the intensity of feeling in the incumbent, Clark did no name calling. In the first place it would not have been effective. Many black citizens would not vote for someone they felt could not work with white folks. Not give in to them in the old pattern but work with them. In the next place it was still dangerous for a black man to inflame the passions of hot-tempered whites who didn't want black people voting in the first place. And certainly not running for office.

I talked to people in Holmes County who as young men and women had voted for Representative Clark and who were now middle-aged to old. When I asked them why they supported him, the majority did not say they voted for him because he was black. The most common answer was that they knew what kind of a man he was. One woman said she voted for him because when she asked him what he could do for her and her family he said, "I can't promise you anything. Except hope." She said, "He brought us hope."

An elderly man said he liked Clark because he "was a character." He told about, as a young man, being at an old black gentleman's house. It was in one of the most remote parts of the county. Clark came by and told the gentleman he was running for representative. The old man, caretaker for an aging white man, was aloof, suspicious, hostile. "Boy, get on away. Ain't none of you niggers gon' do nothing."

Finally Mr. Clark said, "Well, Miss Clark told me if I came up this way to tell everyone hello."

"Who?"

"Miss Annie Clark."

"Miss Annie Clark?" the old man asked. "She taught school here. One of the best teachers we ever had. You say you know Miss Annie Clark?"

"Know her? She's my auntie."

"She yo' auntie for sure? Boy, you can leave now. You don't have to do no campaigning here. We gon' carry this neighborhood for you."

I asked Representative Clark about the incident and he remembered it well. He said the old man took him to the boss's house, introduced them and told the boss this was the one they were going to vote for.

Another man told me about how his family had got to know Representative Clark when he was teaching adult education at Saints Junior College. After the incident over adult education classes, when Clark's response to the board's refusal was considered impudent, he was denied a contract. He was told that he had a job but there was no contract. He got a job at Saints Junior College. At first he was assistant, then director of adult education.

The man told of how his daddy was taking a woodworking class, trying to learn a trade. One night he had a blowout and came in late. The teacher reprimanded him severely. Told him he couldn't stay that night. Later, when Mr. Clark was the director, the same man stopped and helped a woman whose car was stalled on the side of the road. It was cold and there was a baby in the car. His daddy got the car going, then came on to school. He hesitated outside the room, fearing another castigation. Instead, Mr. Clark commended him, knew that he was poor but an honorable man. After that Clark put the students on an honor code. He was a strict disciplinarian but knew these men. Some were illiterate but were deacons or pastors in their little neighborhood churches, good men, heads of households. He knew that hand work on plantations was being phased out with encroaching mechanization. They needed to learn how to make a living other than that of field hand. These were not children and Mr. Clark didn't treat them like children. His program consisted of teaching basic skills. He stressed the importance of screen doors and how to make them, of sanitary outdoor toilet facilities, the value of a clean home. Trades such as carpentry, mechanics, electrical work, and plumbing were taught. Much about these skills required basic reading and writing. Those were taught as well. There were about five hundred adults in the program. When he was running for office the men remembered that "Professor Clark" had treated them with dignity and respect. It didn't hurt. In addition to gaining him political support the program gave Mr. Clark a sense of ministry to the community. He still gets emotional when relating some of the accomplishments of students young in rudimentary matters, old in wisdom and ultimate things. With pride he tells of a Mr. Spann, already beyond the biblically allotted three score years and ten, addressing the graduating class by reading to them a letter from his daughter in Detroit. With hoary locks partially covering his tear-dimmed eyes, eyes telling of years of neglect, hard work, and poor diet, he told his geriatric classmates that his daughter had written him many letters since she left home to go north. This was the first letter he had ever been able to read. Many in the audience joined him with their own tears of joy and triumph. In the telling of the story it is abundantly clear that teacher Robert George Clark was among them.

VI

Winning the election on a rainy day in early November was not the end of the road to the house of representatives for Robert George Clark. There would be challenges. The defeated J. P. Love was determined that Clark would never be seated. Representative Love had not reckoned with the tenacity of the thirty-seven-year-old schoolteacher. Robert Clark had moral resources that would keep him anchored and legal resources of premium caliber.

The chief counsel was a young woman who had come to Mississippi with the civil rights movement and became the first woman to be admitted to the Mississippi bar. Uncommonly bright and well trained as an attorney, she approached the Clark case with religious zeal. Her name was Marian Wright, and she was a graduate of Spelman College and Yale Law School. She is now Marian Wright Edelman, and, as founder and director of the Children's Defense Fund, she has become one of the world's most successful advocates for children.

On her team as a close adviser was the civil rights activist and attorney William Kunstler. Together they met every legal challenge and prevailed. Most of the challenges were frivolous but had to be answered. And in courts not generally predisposed to black litigants. For example, one allegation was that Clark was not a native of Holmes County, the evidence being that he didn't speak with a Mississippi Negro accent. Mr. Clark's Holmes County roots go back to slavery. The accent Love had in mind was the "yasuh, nawsuh" patronizing stance planters expected and generally got from their field hands. Representative Clark's cultivated diction suggested that he must be an outsider, one of the civil rights worker who had come to, in Mr. Love's mind, stir up trouble.

In addition to the legal assistance, the Freedom Democratic Party, various organizations which had been part of the civil rights movement, and individuals let their voices be heard. For example, Mrs. Fannie Lou Hamer sent word to Governor John Bell Williams that if Robert Clark was not seated, she would lead a massive march from the north and Charles Evers would lead one from the south. They would ring the capitol and close it down. By then such messages were not seen as idle threats.

On the day the legislature was to convene, Mr. Clark was still not sure he was going to be seated. The word was that he would be challenged at the last minute and asked to step aside until the matter could be resolved. What he and Attorney Wright did not know was that C. B. "Buddie" Newman, known at the time as an unrelenting opponent of civil rights, had initiated a meeting with Governor Williams, Secretary of State Heber Ladner, and Attorney General A. F. Summers. Twelve years later Buddie Newman told Clark of the meeting. He had told the group that it was his position that Robert Clark had been duly elected by the people of Holmes County, had withstood every challenge, and should be seated.

There was another consideration, one that probably carried more weight than that of being duly elected. Julian Bond had been elected to the state legislature in Georgia and was denied his seat. When the courts ruled in his favor after a bitter struggle, the whole episode thrust Bond into national prominence. They did not want Clark on the national scene because they had denied him his seat.

Although Robert Clark did not know of the meeting which probably stemmed the tide of opposition, it was he who was the deciding vote when Newman campaigned to become speaker years later. Both men had an equal number of signers on their petitions. Newman came to Clark and asked for his signature. Because of Newman's reputation on race, Clark hesitated.

He wanted to get on the inside of the networks of the house and thought this might be an opening. He took the pen from Newman's hand and signed the petition. Representative Clark laughs heartily as he tells it today. "Buddie Newman got down on his knees, kissed the pen I had signed with and said, 'Whoever would have thought a peckerwood would get on his knees to a nigger.'"

Representative Clark says he knew that would cost him the support of a number of white supporters, people he knew to be moderate to liberal on rights for black citizens. He had already been denounced by some of the more aggressive civil rights workers for not being the kind of in-your-face representative they had wanted. He says he believed then, and continues to believe today, that he was serving his people when he signed Newman's petition. When he was first elected, he was sure that his committee assignment would be the Game and Fish Committee, a spot of little influence and power. He wanted to be on the education committee and Speaker Junkin gave him that assignment on his first term. He knew that he would have no substantial influence unless he was chairman. He is convinced that signing Newman's petition clinched the chairmanship. Not only was he reassigned to the education committee but when the chairman, George Rogers, took a position in Washington, Clark became chairman. In that position he was able to effect the legislation he had dreamed of and worked for from the beginning of his tenure. Free kindergartens and compulsory school attendance were two of his favorites. At first each time he introduced the legislation, it would be defeated. "Communism" was still the word of evasion for what people opposed. Clark's kindergarten bill was called a disgrace; it would force little children away from their mothers. Clark's retort was that if a child were still on mother's milk at that age, he was badly retarded and kindergarten wouldn't help him. Compulsory school attendance, which had been repealed in an effort to resist the *Brown v. Board of Education* decision of May 17, 1954, generally didn't make it to the floor for debate. Clark knew his bills would give black children the advantage. Many white children were in private schools anyway. As chairman of the education committee, he saw both bills become law.

Signing Newman's petition, Representative Clark believes, also led to other powerful committee assignments, especially chairman of the Primary and Secondary Education Committee. Being on the rules committee put him in a position of helping to decide which bills would or would not be considered. They made the calendar. He was on the appropriations committee, another commanding assignment.

Clark still laments losing the support and respect of some white liberals who accused him of selling out to rabid racists but feels his record justifies the expedient route he sometimes took. He regrets even more the allegations of some of the civil rights activists that he had sold out to the enemy because he did not introduce the militant measures they espoused. He says he didn't suffer the rejection and insults he endured when he first came only to leave accomplishing nothing. Even his most severe critics will now acknowledge that by biding his time, he was able to accomplish more than if he had taken an offensive which would have led him nowhere.

As we talked, I found the detours and back roads we took getting him and Attorney Wright into the capitol interesting but kept nudging him back to that uncertain and critical first day.

He had been told to come in the front entrance. He had never been inside the state capitol before and it was not clear what was considered front. With Attorney Marion Wright beside him he made his way inside and had to pass the statue of Theodore G. Bilbo. He was stopped there and the photograph that appeared nationwide the next day was of a Negro man and a Negro woman standing beside Theodore Bilbo.

The picture shows two very tense but very determined individuals standing beside the statue of Bilbo, once the prince of darkness to black citizens. A relaxed Representative Clark chuckles as he tells the story today. "This tale may not be original with me but it says a lot about where we are today and where we've come from."

He says that as they stood there Bilbo got on the phone with Senator Jim Eastland, perhaps the most vociferous opponent of civil rights of that day. "Bilbo says, 'Jim, why are you letting that nigger get in the house? When I left Mississippi, I thought I had left it in good hands.'

'Well, Bilbo, when you left Mississippi they didn't have all this civil rights stuff. Now they got Fannie Lou Hamer,

Charles Evers, and Aaron Henry, all the civil rights agitators, and ain't nothing I can do about it. But I'm surprised, Bilbo, that you let him get in here from where you are.'

'Well, Jim. Ain't nothing I can do about it either. They got a nigger fireman down here.'"

Later Clark and Eastland became working political allies.

A friend with me at the time of that interview asked why I didn't at least question Representative Clark for using what she referred to as the "n" word with such abandon, even though it was in the quotes and context. I told her about the time Mr. Clark, Mrs. Clark, and I were walking in the woods at the old homeplace. We came upon a break in the water line. "Honey, we had better call Niggaboy when we get home." He turned to me and said, "Niggaboy is the plumber for the county." He chuckled and added, "He's also chairman of my deacon board."

I suppose I flinched. "You can call him that, Mr. Speaker, but what'll I call him if we meet?"

Mr. Clark smiled—really more of an indulgent grin. When he spoke he seemed mildly impatient. "If you want him to answer, you'll call him Niggaboy. That's his name." After a pause he added, as an afterthought, "Even little children call him that." Mrs. Clark said, "But they use courtesy titles. They always say, 'Mister Niggaboy.'" I remember thinking that I had best bow out. That I was on the verge of being made fun of. Deservedly. Who is patronizing whom here? I saw him cast a soft wink at his wife, then shrug in a sort of "white people still don't understand" fashion. We moved on.

Later on, my friend persisted, saying that it was the duty of everyone to try to clear offensive words from everyday usage. True, but I remembered some words I had recently read in the prestigious *Virginia Quarterly Review*. Words by Leslie Dunbar, one of America's foremost classical liberal thinkers and writers. Mr. Dunbar is a man who wears the "liberal" label with self-respect and need not defer to anyone in his lifelong social activism and intellectual quest for genuine equality and freedom for all citizens. Commenting on the scandalous, hypocritical fashion in which many who claim to be concerned with the nation's welfare hide behind knee-jerk rhetoric instead of immersing themselves in the hard issues, he wrote of "trivial pursuits like political correctness, whose debaters often seem like intellectual children, jousting on their playground, swatting gnats and swallowing camels of war and militarism, poverty and racism, and the degradation of nature. It is time to get serious, and put aside these screens that facilitate our turning away from those problems that truly have our civilization by the throat."

I knew that Mr. Dunbar was not trying to justify offensive words, was not saying that language is of no account. Rather he was saying that justice is based more on what we do than on what we say. The beggar at the cathedral door is not fed by the pious utterances at the altar inside but by the passing stranger who shares a portion of his loaf. I was pretty sure that Representative Clark would understand and concur with Mr. Dunbar's assessment so I left it to others to challenge his reference to "Niggaboy." At least until later when I had gotten to know him better and reminded him of the incident. He laughed and said, "I doubt if we could coach those Holmes kids to say, 'Mister N-wordboy.'" We talked for a minute or so as two bootleg preachers. About moral correctness and political correctness. About what the Bible means when it counsels, not those who say, but those who do.

I wanted to hear more about the scene beside the statue of one of America's most notorious racists. He obliged by telling me more about one of Bilbo's closest facsimiles, Senator Jim Eastland.

"I was having trouble with a project for Holmes County that fit under the Small Business Administration," Mr. Clark said. "An official of the SBA out of the Atlanta office, colored fellow, was giving me the cold shoulder. One excuse after another not to talk to me. I called Jim Eastland and told him the story. 'Whea are you now?' he asked. (Representative Clark does a remarkable imitation of Eastland.) I told him I was in the lobby of the Holiday Inn in Jackson. 'You stay right there, Mr. Clark.' In about fifteen minutes the man I had been trying to reach had me paged. Very cordial. Everything would be taken care of."

This was the same Eastland who in the middle sixties said

there were no voting qualifications based on race, while only 3 percent of his county's Negro population was registered. The same Eastland who said he was against any organization "which indulges, which promotes, racial and religious prejudice, hatred and bigotry" while supporting the John Birch Society, the white Citizens' Council, and every other major white-supremacy organization he knew about. And the same Jim Eastland who said on one occasion, "There's not a Ku Klux Klan chapter in the state of Mississippi."

What brought about the changes between that Senator Eastland and the one who quickly fixed a problem for a black legislator? A part of the answer is the willingness, or ability, of Robert Clark to disregard past transgressions for the sake of today. Many accused Representative Clark of selling out to the establishment. Some called him a moderate who deserted his people. He calls it hustling the system.

In a way Representative Clark was saying something similar to what Mr. Dunbar had said. Namely, that rhetoric is all right but the maintenance of justice need not depend on linguistic fads.

"Let's get you and Attorney Wright inside the house chamber," I said.

"Looking back, it was comical," he began. "By the way," he said as an afterthought. "We got Ole Bilbo moved to the basement."

The time had come for Robert George Clark, grandson of a

slave, to be sworn in as a duly elected member of the Mississippi House of Representatives. The tension was piercing. In
the guest balcony waiting for him to become official were relatives: his aunt and uncle, Henry Clark and Mrs. Doris Clark
of Lexington, a nephew, Robert Steward, who was living with
Mr. Clark at the time, and cousins Howard Bailey, Elaine
Brown, and Swanse Brown. Two friends, Dr. Aurelia Mallory,
president of Saints Junior College, and Mrs. Mary Hightower,
were there as well.

It had been seventy-four years since a nonwhite had been in
the state legislature. The last were G. W. Gayes of Bolivar
County and G. W. Butler of Sharkey County. Both served in
1894. That year closed the political reign of carpetbaggers,
scalawags, and former slaves.

Clark talked for a long time about his first months as a
member of the legislature representing the land where his people had been since slavery days. Few people, white or black,
have such a clear history of their people. It was evident that
talking about it was a nostalgic feast. He mentioned relatives
dating back to his grandfather William Clark, the one who had
talked a man into shooting over his head instead of killing
him in the Big Black River swamp following the infamous
Clinton riots. In a sense he had predicted the future back
when Robert was a little boy. Robert knew there was rejoicing
in heaven when his grandfather told his friends, "That's my
grandbaby standing there beside Ole Bilbo."

He talked of aunts who had taught and nurtured him. Parents, uncles, siblings. His two sons who were fine young men now.

Representative Clark talked of the irony of his first vote, other than those concerning perfunctory housekeeping matters. It was a bill, introduced by Representative H. N. Finnie of Panola County, providing for women to serve on juries. I asked Representative Clark if he voted for or against the bill. Apparently he didn't think the question deserving of an answer.

Once inside the house chamber, Clark remembered, he saw a big, middle-aged man, six-two or six-four, coming at him in a half trot. The new representative, still not sworn in, was sure he was about to be attacked. Instinctively, with all his athletic training and prowess rising within him, the experience of years as a coach of all sports, including the art of self-defense, he dropped his left shoulder and prepared to hit the man. Instead of the anticipated attack the man introduced himself, extended his hand in welcome, and said that if he could help in any way to call on him. Said he was the representative from Neshoba County. Representative Clark chuckled before going on. "Neshoba County, you know, was where the three civil rights workers were murdered and buried in that red clay levee. If I had known he was from Neshoba County I would have attacked him long before he got that close to me." Given the reputation of Klan violence Coach Clark had quit even taking teams to Neshoba County for sports events. Because of the widespread media coverage of the rampant violence there, many Americans looked upon rural Neshoba County as a throwback to the days of troglodytes, a place to be avoided. Robert Clark was at once astonished and pleased that the first act of welcome and civility had come from what would seem the least likely place. Can there any good thing come out of Nazareth?

There seemed to be general confusion as to where he was to sit. He and Attorney Wright were still not sure he would not be asked to step aside. Finally, he was ushered by the representative from Yazoo County to a seat immediately in front, just to the left of the speaker's podium. The seats in the chamber were arranged in pairs. The other chair in that twosome was vacant and Mr. Clark was alone. There was scattered snickering and joking that Clark was now speaker of the house. (Thirty-seven years later that continues to be his seat. There are no more snickers. Now he is speaker pro tem of the house of representatives.)

Being sworn in was a prelude to rejection. He soon learned that much of merit was accomplished at social functions. If Mississippi Power and Light Company gave a dinner for the members of the legislature, he knew it was not to light a candle but to lobby for votes. He attended all of them. And each time he sat alone at a table for eight. "I gained thirty pounds that first session," he laughs. If sirloins and coconut pie were on the table, he had the choice of as many steaks and pieces of pie as he wanted. He says that one night Bill Minor, a fearless veteran journalist, saw Representative Clark sitting alone and came and sat beside him. That seemed to end the long winter of social proscription. Minor became a close friend and advisor on the ways of Mississippi legislation.

On one occasion when "the gentleman from Holmes" was totally ignored when he tried to speak on a bill, he cleaned out his desk and made his hurt and lonely way to his car. Just as he was about to drive away from the capitol for the last time, Bill Minor and Butch Lambert, a representative from Tupelo, a northeast Mississippi town that had long been more progressive than the remainder of the state, stopped him, got in the car with him, and talked for a long time.

"You're doing what they want you to do," one of them told Clark. "Believe me, I've been around here a long time. The opposition to you is fear of the folks back home. Many of the folks here are for you. They knew the day would come when you would be here and they know you won't be the last. They're changing. I know it isn't fair to ask you this but I'm asking you to help them change."

Clark was still unconvinced. As a teacher he had been fired more than once by white administrators; he had left the teaching field for that reason, and he was not going to sit for years being insulted and ignored. Finally Bill Minor said, "They're up there laughing, cheering right now. They've done what they set out to do." With that Clark grabbed the items he had left the chamber with, went back in and began learning how to get things done. He learned well.

Mr. Clark's duties during sessions of the state legislature were a minor part of what he did. Although it would be eight years before Clark had other black colleagues in the house of representatives, by 1970 blacks were being elected to various other offices. Well into the decade the hostility of many whites who were defeated by blacks did not abate. Often the defeated white official would simply walk out, leaving the books of the office but providing no transition. Clark chaired a group that would help newly elected officials. With a foundation grant they hired a lawyer with offices at Tougaloo College. When the grant expired it fell to Clark to carry it on. He had been a teacher all of his adult life. The schools many of those newly elected had attended had not taught them what was necessary for the offices they held. With mock sessions Representative Clark would teach a justice of the peace how to conduct court, constables how to make an arrest and book a prisoner, a school board member what the gist of his duties was.

In addition, since he was the first elected black official since Reconstruction, black candidates and newly elected officials from throughout the state and outside it called upon him for advice and assistance. Constituents from District Sixteen came to him for help in everything from applying for social security to getting their gravel roads graded. Sometimes victims of domestic disputes and violence turned to him for help. There were no boundaries to what people expected; these were people who had never known a sympathetic ear at any level of government. There was no stipend for any of these chores.

He had thought often of marriage but felt it would be unfair to a wife when he was so busy with teaching, coaching, refereeing, and managing the family farm. Now in the legislature he found himself overwhelmed, and for help he resorted to the relief that has existed since Eden. He took a helpmeet, marrying at forty-one.

It was not a whirlwind romance. He had known and had been dating Miss Essie Austin for nine years. He had noticed her at the first teachers' meeting when he returned to Lexington from Leake County. It was not only her beauty and charm he remembers today. She closely favored two boys he had coached and taught in Humphreys County. "You know Joe and Willie Austin?" he asked her at the first break. She smiled and said they were her brothers.

He speaks reverently of her today. "Oh, just beautiful. Round face, big eyes like spotlights. Sweet disposition. Never bossy. Never changed. Devoted to her parents and family." She had graduated from Mississippi Valley State and taught business education in high school. Her father had cut logs to send her to college and when he wanted to buy two lots she owned in Belzoni, she wouldn't have it. Gave him both lots for a house he wanted to build.

Representative Clark speaks with both seriousness and

humor about the marriage ceremony. It was January of 1971. He had been in the legislature for three years, was very busy with the farm, the demands on him as a state representative, and the House of Clark, a furniture business he had in Lexington. It was not a profitable venture but it provided a headquarters for his various activities.

In January of 1971 when the news got around of their marriage there was rude gossip. "So quickly. No announcement. And the wedding was at her father's house. Almost in secret." The rumor, of course, was that Essie was pregnant. Not true but Clark still finds it amusing that the news was treated as if they were teenagers. He says both he and Essie understood the concern of the conservative community. But neither saw any point in a long engagement, bridal showers, bachelor parties, and the like. "I went to Aunt Doris, and together with her daughter we went to the courthouse for a marriage license, drove to Mr. Austin's house in Belzoni and had a brief ceremony by her childhood pastor, Reverend Jody Thurmond."

Mrs. Clark was the help he needed both with his work in the legislature and at home. She was the business manager of the furniture store, and with her secretarial skills she was of immeasurable assistance in the legislature.

Representative Clark turns reflective and sad as he continues with the story. He regrets the long courtship and the postponement of marriage. In seven years Essie was dead, leaving two small children and a heartbroken husband.

The occasion of Mrs. Clark's illness and death was the

most forbidding of Robert Clark's life. What was thought to be an illness of no consequence in the fall of 1977 escalated into a rapid rush to death. She was diagnosed with gallstones and they were removed. Instead of the speedy recovery that was anticipated, the symptoms worsened. Still, neither thought it was anything more than a stall in the recovery from surgery. They were not alarmed. It was Thanksgiving holidays, and during a routine business visit with a neighbor and constituent, Mr. Clark was urged to seek the opinion of a specialist.

All during the Christmas holidays he stayed close to home, letting outside duties wait. His wife was obviously seriously ill and he saw his place as looking after her and the two babies. Robert, Jr., was six years old, Bryant not quite three.

Robert George Clark had learned many of the lines in his role on the stage of legislating. Now another drama had opened. A tragedy. Essie would be cast in the starring role, Robert in the supporting role. Had it been competitive theater, both would have deserved Academy Awards.

Before New Year's he took her to St. Dominic Hospital in Jackson. There the young wife and mother was diagnosed with liver cancer. Given no more than six months to live.

The limited health insurance soon expired but despite mounting bills Representative Clark instructed the hospital to exploit every resource, to spare no expense. M. D. Anderson Hospital in Houston confirmed both the diagnosis and prognosis. There was news about experimental drugs in Africa and Mexico. Representative Clark exhausted every lead but couldn't get access to them. The finale was foredoomed.

During the months leading up to Mrs. Clark's death the routine was the same. Up every morning to get the two boys dressed, fed, and to the preschool at Jackson State, fifty miles away. Back to Ebenezer to fix Essie's breakfast when she wasn't in the hospital. Then to the capitol by 8:30 wearing a suit and tie.

At first he had a helper on the farm. In mid-January the helper left and Mr. Clark couldn't find anyone to take his place. That meant added work.

He was an inveterate hunter. Raccoons, foxes, deer. With thirty hunting dogs and seven American Saddlebred horses he and his friends often hunted on horseback. There was little time for pleasure now. There were also fifty chickens for eggs and meat, the eggs buried in piles of cottonseed to keep them fresh. Twenty-five hogs, over one hundred beef cows.

When Mrs. Clark was in the hospital in Jackson, Representative Clark would leave the hospital at 2:00 A.M., drive to Ebenezer, take care of the animals, and drive back to Jackson to care for his wife, the boys with him. After taking the boys to Jackson State he would walk into the house chambers wearing his suit and tie, his grip in hand. The hardest part, he says, was braving the icy rains of January. A modest bonus was that as a farmer and hunter he had always enjoyed the soft flame of dawn. During those months he could experience that daily.

To help pay his bills he sold the entire crop of hogs.

Supposing that he must have endured those days on the threshold of despair I commended him for such loyalty and hard times. "It wasn't hard," he quickly answered. "They were mine and I wanted to do it and I did it. Not only that, I would do it again." He was silent for a moment. Then he chuckled, "But at my age it would be a hell of a lot harder."

The heart of Robert George Clark was stifled with grief. He would stand and walk. Two angelic little brown boys would steady his gait.

I asked Speaker Clark how long it was until he married again. He knew exactly and answered quickly. Eighteen years, eleven months, and three weeks.

There was a story about Aunt Mae Sula he wanted to pass on. It fit the North African origin of her name. Peaceful. He said Aunt Mae Sula was one he trusted with the children after their mother died. One afternoon when he returned from Jackson, it was getting dark and young Robert was crying for his daddy. Aunt Mae Sula couldn't console him. "That was the last time I ever left them," he said. "Except when they were in day care at Jackson State and then the routine was so tight, they knew exactly where I was. Wherever I went, they went. I ran two unsuccessful campaigns for Congress and they made every stop, every rally with me. In every session of the state legislature they were there." When he went to Harvard they went to Harvard. He even home-schooled them until he was sure they would make it all right without his presence.

It had been thirty-two years since Robert George Clark walked for the first time into the state capitol, confused, not sure which entrance was front and which was back. With Marion Wright, the young attorney not long out of law school at his side, he had been stopped for pictures beside the full-figure statue of Theodore G. Bilbo, the scourge of black Mississippians for four decades. Not assured of being seated, the two of them entered the house chamber where the newly elected Robert George Clark was the brunt of taunts and insults.

Now he was back for the eighth consecutive time. He had long since ceased to be challenged by the likes of Representative J. P. Love. No one challenged him now. The election just past required not one speech or poster. There was no opposition. And on this day, January 4 of a brand new millennium, he would take his place at the podium with gavel in hand to rap to order this first session of the Mississippi House of Representatives of the twenty-first century. There would be no insults now. This time he was speaker pro tempore and would open the session and preside until a speaker was elected. When first he came he was the only African American in the house. That lasted for eight years. Now there were thirty-five. When he had come here in 1968 every seat was taken by males. On this day there were fifteen women, eight of whom were black.

I noted that the representative from the county of my birth, Amite, was black. He had been there twenty years. It was there in 1961 that Herbert Lee was shot dead at a local cotton gin for attempting to register to vote. His killer, never tried, had been a member of the body over which Robert George Clark was now presiding.

The session Speaker Clark was opening was a historical one. Their first order of business, after choosing speakers, was to elect a governor. The antiquated state constitution, passed during the waning days of Reconstruction, required that to be elected a candidate had to receive a majority plus one. There had been two little-known independent candidates, and Democrat Ronnie Musgrove had more votes than Republican Mike Parker but not a clear majority. It was a given that in the house the Democratic candidate would win but Parker refused to concede. A bitter controversy had raged since the November election and today it would be decided.

With Speaker Pro Tempore Robert Clark presiding, formalities for the opening of the first session of the Mississippi House of Representatives of the twenty-first century went routinely. Representative Tim Ford, representing Lee, Pontotoc, and Prentiss counties was reelected as speaker by acclamation.

There was no speculating as to whether or not Representative Clark would be reelected pro tem. He had first been elected to the position in 1991. That time he had serious opposition, including some from black colleagues. One had bitterly denounced Clark and said that his election would be a disgrace to the state of Mississippi. That man was later appointed to a protected state position by Republican governor Kirk

Fordice. Mr. Clark remembers the denunciation with some emotion, not because he couldn't take criticism but because he regretted that his two young sons, with him as usual, had to hear their father maligned by a fellow black legislator.

Recognized by Speaker Ford to nominate a speaker pro tem, Representative Edward Blackmon of Madison County, a man with a law degree from George Washington University who had done graduate work at Tuskegee and Emory, arose to speak. He had been in the house for seventeen years.

Mr. Blackmon began with a text from the book of Exodus, words originally addressed to a people in exile: "I am sending an angel ahead of you to guard you along the way and to bring you to the place I have prepared. Pay attention to him and listen to what he says. . . ."

The words that followed were a compelling tribute to a man who had earned respect, and in many cases personal affection, during the past thirty-two years. There was a reverent quiet in the chamber as Mr. Blackmon continued. Mr. Blackmon reminded the body that Robert Clark had been the first African American representative since Reconstruction and that for nine years he had been the only one, laboring against many odds. Mr. Blackmon, with his fine features, ebony skin, full head of neat peppercorn hair, and calm demeanor exuding confidence, launched into a spirited declamation of the qualifications and deserving moral claim of Robert G. Clark.

Because I wanted to be present to witness the house of representatives electing a governor for the first time in history, and because I wanted to see Robert Clark in action on this historical occasion, I was seated to the side where I could observe the members as Democrat or Republican. Applause was unanimous, party affiliation illegible.

I wondered if the seconding of the nomination would also be by a black colleague. It wasn't. Instead a stylishly coiffured and elegantly dressed white woman with kind eyes and a pleasant speaking voice arose and was recognized. She was Mary Ann Stevens, who had represented Attala, Carroll and Holmes Counties for nineteen years.

In a cultivated and commanding voice she spoke of Robert Clark as "a truly great Mississippian and a friend." She reminded the house that she had proudly nominated him when he was first elected eight years earlier.

Both the speeches were well prepared and well delivered. But everyone seemed to know they were in accordance with established procedure and that Robert Clark's election was not dependent upon the speeches.

When the pretty white lady sat down, acclamation was a hair-trigger response. How different from thirty-two years earlier when this same man was greeted with hostile stares and nearly unanimous disapproval of his presence. And how different from the days of Jackson State's president, Dr. Jacob Reddix, having to go to the Jackson police and plead the case of a student charged with "reckless eyeballing." As I watched I wondered if Speaker Clark's mentor, Dr. Reddix, would believe the scene taking place in the state capitol. I remembered stories Mr. Clark had told me about the designing politeness and amusing machinations of Dr. Reddix with white folks. I recalled an experience I had with him in 1955. I had been with him on several occasions at one or another of the infrequent interracial gatherings held in collegiate circles in those days of rigid racial separatism. On a crowded street in Jackson we met each other, walking in opposite directions. He was holding a folded tabloid in his left hand and as we approached each other he quickly turned to face a shop window as if to see some item and extended his hand, the gesture of friendship shielded from the view of others by the newspaper. That scene had taken place nearly fifty years earlier. Although slow in coming, at least there was some change from the days when a brilliant scholar would have to sneak a handshake on the street to this scene, where one of his students who had loaded manure and run track for schooling was being nominated for speaker pro tem of the state's house of representatives, and by a white woman. No more punishment for "reckless eyeballing."

Representative Clark returned to the dais to be sworn in. "Gracious" Clark had come a long way from voting for the first time in Ebenezer at the age of thirty-seven. Or standing uncertainly beside the statue of Theodore G. Bilbo, flanked by novice attorney Marion Wright, now one of America's most important and well-known women. He was now Speaker Pro Tempore Robert George Clark. Standing with him were the two young sons, now full-grown men, one an attorney, one about to enter law school. His wife, Jo Ann, and other relatives stood proudly with them. With dignity and humility Representative Clark accepted the leadership position his colleagues had just voted on. His acceptance was brief, less than five minutes. But it was time enough to allude to some of the accomplishments that had come about on his watch. He took no personal credit for any of them. Race was not once mentioned. Yet it was implicit in all he said. Health service to the have-nots was high on his list. And "a quality education affordable to every Mississippian without regards for the geographical areas of the state." He made no mention of the fact that forty years earlier, it was the desire of many in this body at the time to abolish public education entirely. He spoke optimistically of programs that must be effected in this and future sessions. One was workforce development, and regarding that effort he returned to his first love—education. His goal was that within a five-year period 60 percent of the state's workforce would be functioning at the level of a high school graduate. An ambitious objective for a state with one of the highest illiteracy rates in the nation. He also emphasized the need for continuing to strengthen the economy, again relating that to education.

While race and the civil rights movement were not mentioned specifically, as I sat in the Mississippi House of Representatives listening to a black man who had integrated this body a short three decades ago I knew he would not be there without the movement. And as I observed I remembered the radicals such as Bob Moses, James Bevel, Ed Brown, Diane Nash, Lawrence Guyot, and numerous others. People who never made it through the electoral process but without whose sacrifice Robert Clark, the moderate, would not be standing there. And without the Robert Clarks playing their current role the fruit of the radicals would lie moldering on the ground. The feat of the moderate is the harvest of the radical. Without both? What? The wrong is that too often the radicals are viewed as rabble-rousers of the sixties instead of the necessary component of social change they were. And the moderates are too often seen as milquetoast bit players on the stage of light opera. Instead, in tandem the moderate may be seen as the limber, the radical as the cannon. Neither is worth much without the other. Robert George Clark has been a significant soldier in the unlimbering, aiming, and firing in the thicket of political warfare.

VII

The audience was applauding the man they had come to hear and praise. Several hundred Jackson State alumni, formally dressed and festive, were gathered in the Grand Ballroom of the Crowne Plaza Hotel in downtown Jackson. They were there to honor the first graduates ever to serve in the Mississippi House of Representatives and the Mississippi Senate—Robert George Clark in the house and Alice Harden in the senate.

Representative Clark, speaker pro tempore of the house of representatives, was reminiscing about his first days on campus. After walking from Ebenezer to Pickens he had caught a bus to Jackson, then the city bus his father had told him would get him to the campus. After getting something to eat and another shirt he was left with thirty-five cents.

The night before leaving home he had walked from one relative's house to another, telling them good-bye and that he was going to college. They had given him small amounts of money. A quarter here, fifteen cents there; to each according as he was prospered. "Here's half a dollar," one aunt had said, planting a vigorous though somewhat somber kiss on his cheek.

In the admissions office he was given a bill for tuition, fees, room, and board. When the young Clark reported that he had no money the testy official asked if he hadn't been told that going to college required money. He knew that he was going to college from high school, just as he had gone from elementary school to high school. Each one was in a different location. The other two, except for books, had required no money.

"I ain't got no money," the nervous farm boy replied.

"Well, telephone your family and tell them to bring some money first thing in the morning."

"My family ain't got no telephone."

"Well, telephone a neighbor and tell them to tell your folks to bring some money."

"My neighbors ain't got no telephone either." He was exaggerating the colloquial grammar for emphasis and the audience loved it.

The admissions officer told him he could spend the night in a vacant room but other arrangements would have to be made come the morning.

When the office opened next morning the disconsolate would-be student was sitting in the corridor reading a two-day-old newspaper. President Jacob Reddix was the court of last resort for difficult cases. Clark was escorted to his office. (A somber mood was evident as the audience considered the plight of a green kid far from home, broke and alone. Most of the alumni at this gala had been students under Dr. Reddix's tenure.)

Representative Clark went on. Dr. Reddix had said, "Young man, I hear you want to go to college but have no money."

"Yessir."

After a lengthy visit Dr. Reddix was convinced that the prospective student was worth a risk. He told Clark the college would give him a work scholarship for half tuition and room and board. It would be up to the student to find weekend chores for the remainder.

"My job was shoveling manure from an abandoned dairy barn. Truckload after truckload. Hour after hour." The skilled orator was about to shift his audience back to a jocular mood. After a pause, sizing up his crowd with a sweeping glance, he continued. "And you know, the experience of that first job has served me well over the past thirty-two years."

Sitting before him were other legislators, men and women, white and black. Some with years in the house and senate, some recently elected. Regardless of their station, Representative Clark was in charge of his audience now.

He continued. "But that's a job a fellow can get tired of right early. So next year I decided to try for an athletic scholarship. Track seemed the logical one for me. I knew I could run. Run fast. I had run after coons and foxes, keeping right up with the dogs."

He described in detail the tryout. "The coach, not much older than the rest of us, called my name and asked me what I ran."

"Track," I answered.

"Boy, I asked you what you run."

"Track. I run track," Clark had repeated. He said he didn't know anything about all the categories. "Hundred-yard dash. Four-forty. Eight-eighty. All that's in meters now, I believe."

He described the growing anger of the coach and his own frustration. "You know how we used to carry on among ourselves. Especially when there weren't white folks around. The exasperated young coach yelled, 'Nigga, I'm asking you for the last time. What do you run?' And I yelled back, 'Nigga, I'm telling you for the last time. I run track!'"

Speaker Clark related the actual trial for each event. He won in every category except the hundred-yard dash. "It always took the dogs further than a hundred yards to warm up for the chase," he said, the laughter growing. The outcome was that Robert George Clark of Ebenezer in Holmes County was the first student ever to get a Jackson State track scholarship.

Before turning serious again he added, "And you know, that second job has served me well, also. Every four years I've had to run again." One jocular old white legislator in the back of the hall called out, "And sometimes, Mr. Speaker, we have had to run when we didn't want to." The others knew what he meant.

It was a good speech. He talked about the contribution Jackson State had made in his own career and in the lives of so many Mississippians. About the importance of education and his wishes for what might be accomplished in the field. About the continuing need for economic development and his own plans for its advancement.

There had already been testimonials of Robert George Clark's contribution to the welfare and advancement of Mississippi. As speaker after speaker, men and women, black and white, droned on about his many accomplishments, I felt a strange and sudden sadness for him. Seeing this son of Ebenezer sitting on this plateau with black and white dignitaries, surrounded by family from as nearby as Ebenezer itself and from as far away as Los Angeles, Las Vegas, and Chicago, accolades flowing and filling the room, I was confused by my own melancholy. I thought of the many honors he had received. But for some reason I thought of the defeats, the loneliness, the tragedies he had known. I remembered something he had once told me in passing. That the most hurtful of all the moods and homesick-inducing emotions was the fact that from the day he arrived at Jackson State he would never again hear himself referred to as "Gracious." Everyone called him that back home. At Jackson State everyone referred to him as Clark. Never Robert. Never Bob. And never Gracious. Clark. It was, of course, a name he was proud to wear. Was it not that of the grandfather, William "Paw" Clark, the one he so adored? The man who had to make the most painful decision possible—whether to run out on the people he was leading in 1875 in Hinds County or to stay and meet death, which in his inflexible Christian commitment he did not fear, but which would be on the immortal soul of his white friend, Jesse Furver? Was it not the name of Henry Clark, his father who had instilled in him the yearning for education and success? Still, he missed "Gracious." In his vanishing youth he still had need of "Gracious."

In any event I was glad I was there. He had asked me to be with him when his alma mater recognized his accomplishments. It was appropriate that I be there.

Now the evening was wearing down and we sat in the lobby of the Crowne Plaza. Just him, Jo Ann, and me. The last of the people who had attended the gala were passing by, smiling and nodding good-bye. Mrs. Clark was still beaming. The two boys, Robert, the lawyer, and Bryant, who was soon to be a lawyer, had said their good-nights.

Our place in the lobby was not far from the almost empty lounge. Near the bar I could see a middle-aged, executive-type man. I took him to be a hotel guest. He was singing an old Kris Kristofferson song of thirty years earlier, popular when the lonely traveler would have been a young man.

"This may be our last good-night together," he slurred. He sang it to some phantom lover, his hand draped in dispirited embrace across the empty chair next to him. "We may nevvv-er pass this way again."

"I believe that fellow is a tad in the grape," I said.

"Uh, huh. Uh, huh."

The nagging I had felt earlier was back. Neither of us could say how the story would end for us, for the end was not yet. Even so, both of us were well beyond the threescore years and ten and we knew the end of our respective stories was drawing nigh.

"Any regrets?" I asked.

"No regrets." He answered without hesitation, his eyes fixed on Jo Ann. I had noticed during the three years of our walk that there was almost always a smile. As if fixed in place.

I inquired about the two losses for the United States Congress.

"Providential," he said. "I didn't know it at the time and I don't deny my disappointment. But it was providential that I didn't go to Washington." He explained that if he had been away he could not have done what he had promised the Clark elders. "I took care of three aunties," he said. "Two in my own home. Helped them live out their days and helped them die. I was single then. I cooked their meals, changed their bed linens, changed their diapers toward the end." He might have added that all the while he was taking care of his aunts he was also taking care of his two little boys. To him that was not something of which to boast. He had told me earlier they were not a responsibility. Not a duty. They were his pleasure. Fifty years earlier he had reluctantly agreed to return to Ebenezer and assume leadership for all the Clark affairs. Nothing having to do with the Clark family was exempt from the pledge. He had heard the supplication of the father and he would not revoke the blessing. There would be no thoughtless warehousing, no dreary nursing home. Each would die in the care and company of her kin.

He talked poetically about how he could tell when it was time to close the house of each aunt and move her into the old homeplace with him. Usually it was when he heard of them giving away all their canning jars. A neighbor would come by, and, as she left, Aunt Drew would say, "I want to give you a few dozen canning jars." There was understanding. Both donor and recipient knew what was being said. No need to verbalize the inevitable. With one aunt it was the spring she didn't plant cut flowers so she would have fresh bouquets to bring to Pleasant Green Baptist Church throughout the summer months as she had done for more than seventy-five years.

"Will you ever run for speaker?" I asked.

"No. Time to move on to something else. I have done everything I can do here."

We talked of some of the rebuffs and defeats he had known over the decades in the house. "There has been some unpleasantness for me in government service. And that's all right."

"But you've made a difference," I said. "You know that."

"We don't like to brag," Jo Ann said, patting him on the knee.

"You've plowed some rough ground, haven't you?"

"Uh, huh. Uh, huh."

We fell to reminiscing about clearing and cultivating new-grounds when we were growing up on small farms in the Great Depression. He in Holmes County. I in Amite.

"Now that's newgrounds, Jo Ann," he said. "Not new ground."

We talked about how not many farmers today know about newgrounds because there are not many wooded areas left to clear. And when it is done today it is with bulldozers, back-hoes, or draglines. With us it was all done by hand. First the trees had to be cut with crosscut saws. No such thing as power chain saws then. The logs had to be dragged from the area with big mules or Percheron mares, harness creaking, their strap-ping backs sweating from the strain. Next the brush had to be piled and burned, the stumps dug or dynamited out. The entire process generally took all winter. When the area was cleared of all tree trunks, limbs, and brush and the stumps removed, the result was called a newground, not new ground, "new" being part of the noun, not an adjective. When every-thing above the surface was gone, that left the feeder roots just under the ground's surface in all directions. The bow-shaped, flexible teeth of a horse-drawn cultivator would sometimes hang under a root, the recoil of the springy metal sending the plow handles back with furious dispatch. Every farm boy remembers being kicked in the pit of the stomach while plow-ing a newground. Representative Clark talked about being so short as a lad that the plow handles would hit him under the chin instead of in the stomach, sometimes knocking the breath out of him. On one occasion he was briefly unconscious, letting the mare drag the cultivator to the end of the row, knocking down the corn as it went. Numerous times he was knocked down, always to get up and go on.

"Yes, plowing previously untilled ground still means trouble," he said.

"And the rotting roots are still under the surface," I added.

"Still up to mischief. Still have to be dealt with," he went on.

We were using metaphors only farm boys would understand. We were agreeing that the ugly scars of racism could abscess from the slightest provocation, taking us back to where we had been, to days we thought were surely gone forever. When he said that the best harvest was always from a newground I knew that he meant that the work he and other black pioneers in the legislature had done was bearing good fruit. That those they replaced had plowed old ground for too long, had become stagnant in the affairs of the body politic.

"Were you ever knocked down in the newground you plowed in 1968?" I asked.

"Came close," he answered. "Or maybe I did get knocked down and didn't even know it. I used to tell my backfield when I was a coach if they didn't know they were down they really weren't. Keep on fighting."

He spoke with some sadness about the breach still existing

between the races in his beloved Holmes County. How some individuals could almost accept blacks as people but not quite. Of how that river will have to be forded by those we will soon leave to continue the journey.

We agreed that at least we have brought them in view of the promised land. We talked of Dr. King's last speech, of how we wished he could have entered and possessed the land.

"Even Moses saw only the hind end of God after wandering for forty years in the wilderness," he said, turning to his preacher mode.

Speaker pro tempore Robert George Clark raised his hand in the manner of a toast. "Here's to you, Will." It was the first time he had ever called me Will. It had always been "Mr. Campbell."

"And to you, Bob." I raised my hand in the same gesture he had. Before, it was Mr. Clark. Or Mr. Speaker. Will and Bob had a nice ring. (The suspension of formalities is sometimes the dawning of brotherhood.)

My walk with the speaker pro tem of the Mississippi House of Representatives was winding down. I knew I would miss someone I had come to know, respect, and love. The walk with this one of my people had been a good one. Yes, my people. I had learned things I didn't know before. One was that the pronoun "my" does not have to do with color. I had had questions answered, suspicions confirmed, vestiges of stereotypes swept away.

"Best we be going," he said to Jo Ann. "It's been a long day."

He got up and left without saying good-bye. I watched them make their way through the lobby, through the yawning doors that opened without being touched, doors that would not have opened for them at all in the not-too-distant past. And then they were out of sight.

Robert George Clark didn't look back. Somehow I knew he wouldn't.

No man, having put his hand to the plough, and looking back, is fit for the kingdom of God. —Luke 9:62

INDEX

WILL D. CAMPBELL

Will Davis Campbell was born in 1924 on an eighty-acre farm in south Mississippi. He attended the public schools of Amite County when he was not working in the cotton fields during the lean years of the Great Depression. Ordained to be a Baptist preacher at seventeen, Campbell briefly attended Louisiana College and served as an infantryman and U.S. Army medic in the South Pacific while still in his teens. After the war he married Brenda Fisher, attended Tulane University, and graduated from Wake Forest University and Yale Divinity School.

First as a university chaplain, then as race relations troubleshooter for the National Council of Churches, and finally as director of an activist organization called the Committee of Southern Churchmen, Will Campbell was among the most conspicuous of white southerners for social justice in the civil rights movement of the 1950s and 1960s.

Since then, he has written sixteen books. *Brother to a Dragonfly*, a Book of the Month Club selection, was named by *Time* as one of the most notable works of nonfiction of the 1970s, and the *New York Times* called it one of the top ten books of 1977. That book won a Christopher Award and the Lillian Smith Book Award and was a finalist for the National

Book Award. *The Glad River*, a novel, won the Friends of American Writers first prize for fiction. *Providence*, a history of one square mile of land in Holmes County, Mississippi, from the Choctaw period to the present, was awarded the Richard Wright Prize for Literary Excellence.

Among Campbell's other titles are *Up to Our Steeples in Politics*, a critique of modern religion; *Forty Acres and a Goat*, a memoir; *The Stem of Jesse*, an account of higher education desegregation in the South; *The Convention*, a parable of the Southern Baptist Convention; and *And Also with You*, a biography of the Episcopal bishop Duncan Gray, Jr.

Campbell is also the subject of two books: Thomas Connelly's *Will Campbell and the Soul of the South* and *Will Campbell: Radical Prophet of the South* by Melvin Hawkins. A PBS documentary on his life, "God's Will," was shown nationally in August 2000.

Among Campbell's recognitions have been the Alex Haley Memorial Award for Literary Distinction, state awards in both the arts and the humanities from the governor of Tennessee, the Lifetime Achievement Award of the Tennessee American Civil Liberties Union, and honorary degrees from several American universities. In December 2000 he received the National Presidential Humanities Medal.

Will and Brenda Campbell have two daughters and a son and four grandchildren. The Campbells live on a farm near Mt. Juliet, Tennessee.